40877

HQ
769
.W695

Wiener, Daniel N
    Training children in self-discipline
and self-control; or, How to be good
parents and teachers without at all
times pleasing, indulging, or giving
love, by Daniel N. Wiener and E. Lakin
Phillips. Prentice-Hall [1971]
    x, 257 p.

    1.Discipline of children. 2.Self-
control. 3.Children—Management. I.Phil-
lips, Ewing La   kin, 1915- jt. auth.
II.Title
649.6   HQ769.W695

                         74-157764

DISCARD

TRAINING CHILDREN
IN
SELF-DISCIPLINE
AND
SELF-CONTROL

Other books by the authors:

Short-Term Psychotherapy and Structured Behavior Change
Discipline, Achievement and Mental Health

Training Children in Self-Discipline and Self-Control

or How To Be Good Parents and Teachers Without at All Times Pleasing, Indulging, or Giving Love

by Daniel N. Wiener, Ph. D.,
and E. Lakin Phillips, Ph. D.

Prentice-Hall, Inc.
Englewood Cliffs, N. J.

Training Children in Self-Discipline and Self-Control or How To Be Good Parents and Teachers Without at All Times Pleasing, Indulging, or Giving Love
by Daniel N. Wiener, Ph.D. and E. Lakin Phillips, Ph.D.
Copyright © 1971 by Daniel N. Wiener and E. Lakin Phillips
ISBN 0-13-926253-9
Library of Congress Catalog Card Number: 74-157764
Printed in the United States of America • T
Prentice-Hall International, Inc., London
Prentice-Hall of Australia, Pty. Ltd., Sydney
Prentice-Hall of Canada, Ltd., Toronto
Prentice-Hall of India Private Ltd., New Delhi
Prentice-Hall of Japan, Inc., Tokyo

To P, who proves daily
that there are also other good ways
to rear children

To the Staff of SCE

INTRODUCTION Many more parents than psychologists have considered writing a guide on how to be a good parent or how to raise children well. But then hundreds of thousands of Americans, if not millions, also believe that they have a good novel locked inside of them, awaiting only enough free time, and a pill to produce instant willpower, to get written. Professionals who work with children also talk endlessly of their ideas and observations, better than any on the market, that they will publish—sometime.

Producing this plethora of superb (though unwritten) books founders on the rocks of distraction, indolence, incompetence—and lack of discipline. And of these, lack of discipline appears to be foremost. With self-discipline even a microscopic talent can flower into skill, productivity, and effective writing. Because of the inherent variability of all human productions as we judge them, only a miniscule amount of the writing that would result would be considered good, but at least the aspirations of the authors would have been fulfilled.

We are not reluctant to join the ranks of parents and professionals who think that they have something to offer society by way of views on how to rear its young. The marketplace of interested consumers is the proper place to test such views when they are presented in testable form. "Testable form" is a key concept in all scientific enterprise and is surely relevant to counsel about the rearing of children. It means simply that the views of the author (whether he is experimenter, teacher, philosopher, psychologist, or whatever) are expressed in procedures which can be applied to children in standard ways, observed objectively, and judged to determine whether the suggestions work as described. Our views will be stated explicitly and practically so that they can be tested by readers.

Furthermore, precision and consistency mark the views of a mature professional man or scientist—as distinguished from the immature ones and ordinarily also from the common-sense views of experience-wise or clever laymen. The most effective parent—or teacher, lawyer, physician, clergyman—has character, we say, meaning some central principles, a tempered amalgam of values, experiences, and intellectual activity, which can be effectively applied with consistency when situations are similar, or adjusted according to differences in problems.

This approach will distinguish our counsel, we hope, from that of the newspaper advice columns which provide counsel from off the top of somebody's head, which is clever, legally acceptable, and sometimes funny. We will attempt to do better in this way: we will try to describe, and to apply with precision and consistency, some *central principles* about training children which, once learned, can be applied to a far wider range of problems than any book can cover. Our goal is to help teach parents, and others who have responsibilities in the rearing of children, how to train children so that the goals of the parents (or others) can be achieved.

Finally, we take a stand on what some crucial goals in child-rearing should be. They furnish the title for this book. "Self-discipline" we take to mean the characteristic of a person which determines his effectiveness in realizing his chosen goals, whatever they may be; that quality which makes the human machine efficient in achieving its purposes. By "self-control" we mean the child's ability to take responsibility for his own behavior, success, or failure, and to assume the direction of his life toward his goals.

We will not attempt to define the personal goals that human beings might choose, although we probably tend to influence our children, students, and clients toward humanitarian and long-term satisfactions. But we do unqualifiedly set for ourselves the aim of encouraging people to choose *some* goals that seem very important to them, and to work toward these goals as well as they can. We believe and would teach that the most effective way of achieving such goals is through taking responsibility for the control of one's life, and disciplining oneself to utilize one's resources as powerfully as possible in pursuit of those aims. This, then, we take to be the prime training function of the parent—or anyone else seeking to educate or train children. Whatever other influences are important—such as love, environmental resources, encouragement, acting as model—they can be evaluated in terms of their contributions to the making of an effective human being.

What about personal happiness in this scheme of things? We believe that it stems from a sense of personal effectiveness in achieving one's goals, what one wants from life; that self-discipline and self-control lead to achievement, and achievement to satisfaction, happiness, or whatever one may call a state of equanimity about one's life. We speak here of achievement not necessarily of material goods, or of power, or of professional status, but merely of whatever one sets before oneself as most important to accomplish or simply to be like.

What of spontaneity and pleasure? Does self-discipline mean being duty-bound, compulsive, and calculating? Does it mean being joyless? Far from it. Self-discipline means being able to mobilize effectively to reach one's goals *whatever they may be.* If spontaneity is one of the goals, and it does not prevent reaching other important ones, that can be included as a goal of the rearing.

Training the child in how to assume responsibility for reaching his goals, and how to make effective use of his abilities in doing so becomes, then, the purpose of child-rearing in all settings. Such training need not be highly developed and calculated. Most parents are not highly self-conscious about their methods in raising their children, and most children seem to develop good enough habits to live as adults without serious trouble inside themselves or with their environment. But many human beings do have serious troubles inside or out. And psychological counseling, in order to make important changes occur, seemingly must make parents acutely self-conscious of how they handle matters poorly when they do, and what they can do instead, in order to succeed. So intensifying an awareness of problems and solutions becomes a vital goal of this book.

Furthermore, few human beings utilize their re- sources to anywhere near their maximum. The limit of potential human achievement is nowhere in sight. Waste is enormous. What we loosely call "mental illness" can be considered a by-product of disorganization and self- defeating habits. It seems certain that if we could learn how to rear children to set and successfully to achieve their goals, rates of "mental illness" would be significantly reduced. This, too, is an important purpose of effective child training.

CONTENTS

TRAINING CHILDREN
IN
SELF-DISCIPLINE
AND
SELF-CONTROL

PART I

BACKGROUND AND PRINCIPLES

CHAPTER I

The Importance
of Self-Discipline

IF THERE IS not an old Chinese proverb like this one, there should be: He who seeks to be loved by giving gifts will in the end perhaps receive gifts; he who seeks to be loved by turning away dislike will in the end perhaps not be told of dislike; he who does not seek love but finds his own way will in the end perhaps be loved for himself.

Parents, teachers, all who are responsible for training the young—rearing, raising, educating them—face the same primary problem: How are children to be trained to function well as independent human beings, in the sense that they can make decisions and otherwise guide and control their own lives, and be able to please themselves in the broadest and longest-lasting ways, without harming others?

What is the importance of self-discipline? It lies in the freedom of choice that self-discipline provides. It—and it alone—can give the child his freedom. It is the tool with which to fashion a life that pleases him; it gives him the power to sculpture the shape of his being. Self-discipline, which encompasses self-control, is the means by which the human being gains command of his abilities and uses them to carve a satisfying life for himself from his environment. He creates of himself a work of art, or an efficient machine, or whatever image he wishes. But it is he who must shape himself according to his own lights if he is ever to find satisfaction. Unhappiness, we believe, grows from a sense of inability to control the forces that shape one's life, or inability to use one's resources well, beginning or ending with a tendency to blame other people or powers outside oneself for one's ineffectiveness. And of these forces blamed, first come parents and second teachers.

Are parents and teachers always to be blamed when children lack self-discipline?

Taking Responsibility

For the victim, *blaming others* for his deficiencies and unhappiness is irrelevant, even if parents (or teachers) could have done better. We have never talked with parents who did not want to love their children. There are monsters of all types in the world, and parents who hate their children do exist. But far more often the parent simply does not know how to combine his love with effective training, and ends up feeling helpless, hopeless, angry, or frustrated—a Samson shorn of his ability to exercise the mighty powers he knows he must possess to help his offspring develop strongly and well. An eight-year-old boy says that he hates his mother who refuses to buy him a fire engine. He has succeeded before in this way—or by crying—and so he expects to again. If she then buys the engine, she increases his expectation that he can get what he wants in the future by saying that he hates her or by crying. If she does not buy the engine, she may feel guilty or depressed because he says he hates her, feeling that she does not love him properly or enough.

She has not learned—perhaps *discovered* is a better word—that to succeed in raising her child to an effective adulthood she must learn two roles, not just one: how to convey her love *and* how to train him well.

If she refuses the fire engine for good reason—it may be an extravagance in her budget, he may have purposely damaged one like it, he may be able to save money to buy a fire engine himself in two or three weeks—and tells him why, she contributes to his training. Thus she translates the love that she has for him not just into pleasing him as much as possible but also into contributing to his future strength and happiness.

The bedrock of theory that our view of training rests upon is that the adult who feels most fulfilled is he who has learned most effectively how to *earn* his rewards through the exercise of his own powers. First he learned to want what brings him fairly long-lasting, stable pleasure, then he learned how to get what he wants through his own efforts in ways he can use all of his life. He is the child who was told why he could not immediately have the fire engine, and how to gain it in the future. He learned through necessity to accept his mother's decision, to test the lastingness of his interest, and to develop responsible methods of gaining what he wanted *most*—from anyone.

The child who, by tears, withholding love, or expressing hate, won over his mother to buy the engine learned how to gratify his impulses, and in a way that will earn him little or nothing in the adult world—unless he finds a wife who is subject to the same techniques of control.

The Parents' Role

Love Is Not Enough (by Bruno Bettelheim, Glencoe, Ill.: Free Press, 1950), an apt book title, suggests a facet of the problem. How can love be translated into effective training? For love can prompt the parent to improve his ways of raising his children. It can be the energizer that will lead parents to spend time, effort, and money to learn how to better their ways of rearing their young. And, in backlash, bad methods may well curdle love on either side.

The parent caught up in a terrible tangle of misunderstanding and conflict with an adolescent boy or girl may find his love shriveling. "How," he may ask, "can I love a son who swears at me, tries to shove me around, or steals my wallet?" A mother may feel her love freezing when she discovers birth control pills in her seventeen-year-old daughter's drawer or sees her slipping into the house at two or three A.M. despite lurid threats of punishment.

Such parents, trapped by ineffective methods of dealing with their children's problems, may well almost forget what their love for their children once felt like. They may feel the stirring when they or the children are away on a vacation and communication is vague, or when they see them perform before strangers, or when they look in on them asleep. But the concrete daily contact with conflict is more than their love can bear.

The child, too, can forget love. The son of thirty, living in the same city as his parents, refuses to call or visit them because they have refused him money to buy a car—for the first time actually refused him, despite his strongest pleadings. Or the twenty-five-year-old daughter calls Mother weekly to cry that her husband does not want to visit her family for their vacation and that therefore, he does not love her.

But how is a parent to cope with problems of child-rearing? Isn't common sense enough? Don't children go through "stages" that they outgrow? Who are the experts? And how come *their* children don't turn out so well? A study of psychoanalysts' children, for example, indicated that they also had severe problems.

Parents are not born with the aptitude to train children to become effective, happy adults. Most parents, however, do fumble their way to fairly successful methods. Ideally, perhaps, research will distill the best ways of the parents and provide knowledge to professionals, who will teach prospective parents while they are still youths in school. Or professionals, in addition to parents, will train groups of schoolchildren in methods of using their abilities well and achieving satisfaction.

Meanwhile, millions of parents, themselves cripples by *their* poor training in childhood, raise children who will train *their* children just as poorly, and for the same reasons—and so on with subsequent generations.

How can we interrupt this process? How can the mother who was "spoiled" avoid "spoiling" her children, and they theirs, and so on and on? We start wherever we can in the available generation—with parent or child or grandchild—in whatever ways we can, with whoever can be exposed to help.

What Kind of Training?

What kind of help is required? We have already developed the theoretical grounds for it.* It is not more superficial or less effective than so-called "depth" methods, which are indirect and take enormously longer. In fact, research suggests that it produces better and longer-lasting results than other methods.

This kind of help can be simple, direct, and as useful as any. It is founded in experience and research. Best of all, it is almost immediately *testable.* That is, you need not wait for six months or a year or two to pass before seeing results. You need not assume that you first have to poke in the murky depths of your or your child's personality before you can take effective action.

What we will be suggesting throughout the book is that you *try* this or that approach, or that you find a psychologist who is willing to recommend some specific action as a solution and let you judge the results for yourself—and over a period of weeks, and not many months or several years.

For we view training children to become self-disciplined and capable of controlling and directing their own lives in the same light as training any human beings in other habits

---

Short-Term Psychotherapy and Structured Behavior Change, by E. Lakin Phillips and Daniel N. Wiener (McGraw-Hill, New York, 1966).

or skills: first one decides what is to be taught, then one sets about to teach it as effectively (that is, in as short a time and with as long-lasting results) as possible. Parents, then, are teachers, educating their children as best they can in how to become the kind of adults who can choose and gain what will give them greatest satisfaction for the longest time.

Choosing Goals

The question of the quality of goals must be raised. Should parents train their children in how to choose and gain whatever they want? In part, this problem involves personal attitudes which we cannot cope with fully here, but as a matter of principle, we do not want to train children in how to obtain trivial or impulsive goals. We assume that they would not satisfy for long and their overall effect would be to produce a restless, unhappy adult. So we assume that effective training should include the ability to choose goals which will provide a deep and lasting sense of satisfaction with one's life—without harm to others, if not actually contributing to their welfare. This, we hope, will give some dignity and importance to our training approach, distinguishing it from the mere manipulation of others or one's talents to gain narrow, short-lived pleasures.

So we return finally to "self-discipline" and "self-control" as perhaps the most vital goals in the training of children because they are such powerful vehicles to the achievement of other goals. There are many such goals, however: to love widely and well, to earn a living, to become educated in the fruits of civilization, to enjoy the arts, to help fellow human beings, to wield power well, to cultivate one's body, and on and on. We have chosen self-discipline and self-control because they would appear, above all others, to make the others achievable. They are the organization of your powers (self-discipline) and direction of your powers (self-control) to achieve your purposes. They permit you to get where you want to go.

If you train your child in self-discipline, he can organize to their maximum the resources he possesses—to study, to work, to create, to socialize, to save, to influence, to play or any other purpose. With self-control (and we mean control and direction of oneself, *not* inhibition) your child chooses and pursues his goals without having to depend upon others. He sets his course and steers himself; he is both an efficient machine and its operator. He gains satisfaction from exercising his powers near their maximum in ways and for goals that please him. If these goals turn out to be unsatisfactory, he chooses and pursues others with similar efficiency until he finds those which do please him. He has learned the most powerful habits for personal fulfillment that you can teach him. And you can know, then, that you have done well a job that is crucial to your child's happiness.

Is Overachieving Possible?

But should man not be more than an efficient machine or a work of art? Working hard to use himself well, might not your child grow up "soulless," unfeeling, insensitive?

There is no incompatability at all between the view we have sketched of *effectiveness in working toward one's goals,* and soul, feelings, or sensitivity. Achieving one's goals can never, we believe, be overdone. The very idea of "overachievement" seems meaningless. There should be no limit on working toward the virtues, whichever one may wish, such as love, honesty, creativity, kindness. Nor on achievement and efficiency in the use of oneself. Why should one ever need to impose limits on developing his skills or virtues? Life will impose limits, of course, as will one's native aptitudes and physical capacities. But within the limits imposed by conflicting goals (for example, choosing how to divide time between a job and an artistic interest), physical health, and talent, one cannot, we believe, suffer from too much control, organization, direction, efficiency, in using one's skills to reach one's goals.

What is sometimes called "overachievement" (how can you ever really achieve better than your abilities?) means usually that you are upset and unsatisfied by your present performance and seem compelled by some inner force to overwork to the point of exhaustion and continuous unhappiness. This state is not caused by achievement beyond your capacities, however, or by an excess of self-discipline. It usually means that you have chosen goals which you do not like or which are unrealistic; that you feel driven, not freely choosing; that you do not do other things you would prefer.

The child who has been trained to choose and take responsibility for his own goals, to gauge his success by his own satisfaction, and to direct and use his capacities with maximum efficiency is unlikely to be called an "over-achiever." That label is usually applied to unhappy people.

CHAPTER II

Parental Hopes, Goals, Roles

ALMOST ALL PARENTS want to be good parents. There are few who are so twisted that by no stretch of an observer's imagination can good intention be perceived beneath a cruel or unfeeling exterior. For the sort of people who would read this book, in any case, there are probably no exceptions to the presence of good intentions about training children to become independent, achieving and happy—however ineffectual, fumbling, or even harmful their efforts may turn out to be.

How, then, can one account for the poor results often produced, compared with the high hopes? Are the hopes *too* high? Is it perfection rather than realistic expectations that are sought? Is the parents' influence certain to be less powerful than they would wish? Are children bound to rebel against parental goals and methods whatever they may be?

Consider the view of this book: that self-discipline and self-control are the best ways, perhaps the only ways, to produce independent, happy, self-fulfilling human beings, but that to some these habits for successful living may come easier than to others, even to the point of seeming inborn, while others must work hard at gaining them.

Is Training Necessary?

The trainer's—the parent's—job, then, is determined by the status of the child. That child who is already reasonably satisfied and achieving—in other words, who is able to direct himself well—needs a minimum of parental help, perhaps only when he asks for it or is obviously stymied or can profit from special resources he cannot find for himself but which the parent can provide.

Nor should the parent try to impose goals on the child who is getting along satisfactorily with reasonable ones of his own. The way the parent leads his own life will be a model for the child which will almost always influence the child to some extent, even if it simply stands before him to be observed.

Or the parent may gently nudge the child in this direction or that, and leave it to the already progressing child to accept what he wants from the parent.

But for the great majority of children, we believe that the parent's role can usefully be a more active one. Most children, we feel, are either lost and confused about which of many stimuli in their lives to choose and follow, or are following random or poorly chosen paths that frustrate or defeat them in their search for satisfaction, or simply use their abilities and interests poorly as they move along in their lives.

It is with this large mass of children that parents can be most useful in helping them find ways to act and use themselves that will please them. Why should parents not take such a part in the rearing of their young? All other animals do what they can to help their young avoid danger and grow up well. True, the human animal is far more complex than others, and the path of growing up well is far more difficult to specify when values, personality, and achievement are involved than when the only criterion is to avoid death or physical danger. But the principle is the same. In the case of the human young we only have to extend it to include these more complicated ideas of what growing up well means.

If parents are too anxious about the matter, if they are cowed into thinking that they should leave their children alone to grow up as they will, they will have no chance to reduce the crippling effects that children do suffer when left alone, as well as when badly treated. Just as good public health practices with children reduce the damaging effects of amoebae, spirochetes, and bacteria, so can good early training reduce damage from nature's psychological dangers.

It is a strange philosophy, indeed, that says the best child-training is the least, that implies nature should be left to its own course with children psychologically, as if a process of natural selection which humanitarians reject in the biological field were the best principle to follow in the psychological field.

Many parents feel very uncomfortable about raising their young, the more so as they have been made self-conscious about what they are doing by psychologists and others who attribute childhood—and adult—problems to the way parents treat their children.

It is true, of course, that parents *are* probably the most powerful influence on their children's behavior, at least up to the school years and perhaps until the years 8 to 12, when children move to closer relationships with groups of their friends.

But this parental influence can be good or bad. The fact that it is sometimes misguided or produces harmful later effects is surely no good reason to try to suppress it and to hope that the child will find his own way—any more than the practice of medicine should be abandoned because it has produced such horrors as blood-letting for respiratory disorders and brain-cutting for psychological troubles.

What is desperately needed is *better* child-training. Slowly, psychological research seems to be pointing the way. Painfully, with many errors, a science is forming which can help parents to take effective action in rearing their children well.

Parents' Worries

Many parents worry that their own strong feelings and personal hangups will ruin their children. Then they try to avoid guiding their children or feel guilty after they do and try to undo what they have done. Or they indulge their children to make amends for being tough or getting angry or doing something in their own personal lives that they are ashamed of.

Consider this different view of the parent's role, however: Parents are *teachers* of their young, and to be good teachers they need to know *what* to teach and *how* to teach. They need to know this, not in a highly technical sense, but only sufficiently so that children will learn what they need. In fact, since all animals "teach" their young, the skill cannot be highly technical in the sense of requiring high intelligence or formal training. Here, however, we are considering mainly how to provide what is lacking, how to correct deficiencies. To do that efficiently calls for us to use all we know technically about teaching skills. In the world of the other animals, nature presumably is less interfered with than in man's world by artificial obstacles such as worry and theories—and the deficiently trained simply die young.

With this view of their role firmly in mind, parents can begin to rid themselves of many irrelevant concerns, such as: Will my children love me if I don't show love to them all the time? Will they hate me if I don't let them look at television before they do their homework? Will they be psychologically damaged if I leave them at home when they cry to be with me? Will they hate me and piano-playing if I insist that they practice? Will they grow up neurotic if I don't let them have that toy they're crying for? Will they be nervous for life if I slap them occasionally?

Why are all of these problems irrelevant when we think of the parent as a teacher? Because the role of a teacher is to teach as well as possible what he is charged with teaching. Thus the parent need look only to the goals he sets for himself and how best to reach them.

Many and varied goals are possible. Some are fairly universally agreed upon, such as honesty, fair-mindedness, and kindness. In any case, the principles for reaching them are the same as for reaching any others. They involve applying the principles of learning and good teaching to child-training.

Certain habits (goals) also are basic to all other goals: self-discipline and self-control, with their related characteristics of taking responsibility and being flexible and objective and active in trying to solve one's own life's problems.

Self-conscious or Spontaneous?

The parent, then, sets goals for himself and tries to reach them. Not that the process must always be planned and self-conscious. Most parents set about their job of child-training without such conscious direction. But trying to do the job without *some* awareness means at least less efficiency and at worst the poor results or disappointments that so often suddenly strike the parents of teen-agers when changes are much harder to produce than with younger children.

What we are saying is that self-consciousness and planning are necessary methods for changing yourself when spontaneity and natural or impulsive actions get you into trouble or do not move you toward your goals. When, and just as soon as, you can trust and satisfy yourself that you are training your children well, and as soon as your ways have become stable and reliable—when you have, in other words, good habits of training your children—you can become spontaneous again, this time because spontaneity does well for you. You can then depend upon your habits, your own learning and discipline and character, to do a good job of training your children near, at least, to your best.

Perhaps the greatest curse our language puts in the way of improving your behavior is its kiss of approval for the word "spontaneity"—regardless of whether the spontaneity leads you to ignore or hate, beat or confuse, deceive or buy off, tease, bully, or indulge your children—or whether it leads you to love and guide, explain and lead, let penalties fall naturally and rewards be earned, in your rearing them.

We suggest that you consider, as parents, how to make yourselves into the best teachers of the young that you can. You may, like a few classroom teachers, seem to have been born effective. But if you are like the great mass of teachers—and other skilled workers of all types in our society—you will gain from working hard at becoming as good as you can be at your job.

This is not to say that you need be highly self-conscious, fearful of making mistakes, super-cautious, compulsively planful. These are *not* the marks of a good teacher—or any other good worker. There can be a joy and freedom in learning, then practicing your skills well, the greatest kind of satisfaction—like mastering the simpler skills of golf, sewing, cooking, or investing—only usually far more rewarding when the job is done well.

The *methods* of effective training will be discussed in a later chapter. Here we will discuss parental expectations, goals, and roles.

Other Roles

If the parental role is primarily that of a teacher, he should learn to do it well and, if he does it well, his other roles as model, inspirer, and lover of his children will fit in.

Just as the teacher can teach his children well even if troubled personally, can do a good job even if unable to inspire them with moving messages, and can be a capable technician even when he has no deep love for them individually (communal child-rearing can work well, and even teaching *machines* can teach well)—so can the parent rear his children well if he follows the principles of learning and good teaching, even if he is not a good model, inspirer, or lover.

It would be better if all parents did possess these latter qualities. They would almost certainly enhance the teaching of children. But it is more practical and useful for parents to focus primarily on *what* they would teach their children and how they wish to train them, and how best to reach these goals, rather than on the vaguer and much less achievable concepts of inspiration, love, and example. These qualities also will often fall into place when goals, methods, and results are successfully made the main focus of efforts.

No matter which role the parent takes, however, it is vital that he check his *results.* Our message repeatedly will be to focus on *results,* with full regard to goals and methods and their implications. If you concentrate *only* on perfecting your love or example or preachments to your child, you may assume that, if your results are poor, it is because you are not performing well enough in one of these roles. You would then try all the harder to love, set a good example, or convince. You would thus be limiting yourself to some predetermined idea of what is the best (most successful) way to be a good parent, instead of giving your attention to results and the best method of achieving them. You might blame yourself for not being loving enough, for example, when a few simple limits and a bit more firmness might produce good results in whatever it was you were aiming for.

It is futile to concentrate on perfecting *means* instead of on accomplishing results and choosing any reasonable means that work best.

Surely we would not reject love, inspiration, or example

as strong influences in training children, but they are seldom enough. When the parent tries and tries and tries to make them work in the face of obvious ineffectualness, what sense does it make to persist when more powerful or effective tools may be at hand?

For powerful methods to shape behavior are at hand. They are not antagonistic to nor exclusive of these other parental roles; they are merely different. They are the tools with which learning, training, teaching, research, and experiment have provided us, and we would be foolish to ignore them. They are the most effective ways we presently know to train children to reach the desired goals, any goals. These methods will be discussed in a later chapter.

A Democratic Relationship and Freedom

But should not every human being have a sacred right to grow up as he will, to determine his own fate? "Within some kind of limits," one might quickly add, since physical survival is one goal all parents would agree is their universal, invariable responsibility. You would never agree to allow a baby or child the freedom to starve to death, to die or be damaged by disease, to be badly beaten by other children, to wander into the street, to eat a nutritionally deficient diet.

There are other restrictions on freedom, widely but not universally accepted, that involve avoiding less serious psychological, behavioral, and physical dangers such as eating somewhat inadequate diets, unnecessary exposure to illness, refusal to defecate for several days, total withdrawal from social activity, or damaging nervous habits (for example, thumb-sucking that is deforming a mouth or scratching that is opening infected wounds).

In all of these situations, the serious and the less serious, with parental intervention and the use of the best training methods, the parent can help the child to survive physically and psychologically.

But there are much less clear areas of problems where parental intervention is more controversial. Should a parent exercise all his power and skill to get his child to master a musical instrument, to drink milk (when he is not suffering from dietary deficiency), to eat all the food placed before him, to engage in physical activities, to eat meals at regular times, to speak courteously to his parents and others or not to swear, to restrict his television viewing, not to bully younger siblings, to keep his room in some fair order, to go to sleep at a reasonable hour?

Each parent will have to decide for himself what goals are most important. He cannot effectively control and train the child in everything at once. As a practical matter, his intervention should be reserved for the matters he considers most important. He should also keep in mind the total family and home situation and what behavior is most necessary for the overall welfare.

But we would urge also that certain goals be made primary for the purpose of providing the child with the tools (habits) that are necessary for him to enjoy and profit from freedom. These might be considered universal for psychological well-being, much like the necessities for physical survival, where parental training is clearly advantageous, if not essential.

Can training a child in self-discipline, self-control, and responsibility cause damage to him by restricting good spontaneous development?

The parent who trains his child in this way is developing the child to exercise freedom as broadly and satisfyingly as possible. That child is *not* free who is confused, distractable, uncertain, and diffused, and who therefore goes about in circles for years, perhaps all of his life, wasting himself and his opportunities, even feeling miserably *un*free because he never seems to be able to accomplish what he wants to or, indeed, does not even know what he wants.

That child *is* free who has been born to, has been

unwittingly shaped to, or, far more likely, has been purposely trained to, choose his goals and then to move toward them in reasonably efficient ways through good habits of working for what he wants.

It is assumed that in politics it takes an educated, mature citizenry to make democracy work well, that uneducated or primitive peoples seem generally not to handle it successfully. So it would seem to be also in the home. In the training of the uneducated, immature young, it seems obvious that the parent should protect, guide, and teach, and that a permissive system or a completely democratic one where the parent has no special voice simply produces, as nature does, a higher rate of fatalities, crippling, and ineffectualness than does man's best efforts. It seems apparent, too, that as in nature physical strength and skill are almost always advantageous, in child-rearing psychological strength and skill (ability to use oneself well) can only be advantageous and never disadvantageous.

So we come to this: that the democratic relationship need not rule out—indeed, will thrive on—the kind of education that makes people (children) best informed and most capable of achieving their purposes.

What these purposes are and how they are chosen is another matter. Surely there is no advantage to the parent or child for the parent to insist (other than for *practical* reasons such as distance to lessons, cost, or obvious skills or lacks) that the child be trained in dancing instead of a musical instrument, in music instead of athletics, in science instead of the arts, in a profession instead of a skilled trade, in social skill instead of solitary pursuits.

It is in the choice of goals that the democratic relationship between parent and child flowers, and, within the broadest practical limits, children should be free to follow their inclinations, if they have any. They can and should experiment as broadly as they wish. But for those skills that are necessary to function with maximum freedom in our society, the parent, we believe, should take responsibility: the basic skills of communication and calculation and of surviving physically, socially, and psychologically; and of goal-setting, self-discipline, self-control, and responsibility—all essential to the attainment of any goals.

Feedback

One important advantage of a democratic relationship between parent and child, within the limits outlined above, is that it encourages "feedback" between them. That is, when the child feels that his views are respectable and respected, he can argue with his father and mother, he can try to correct them when he thinks they are wrong or ignorant about him, and he has a chance to be convinced of his incorrectness. In this way, when the parent truly is misinformed, insensitive, or mistaken about his child—and is open-minded enough to learn and change—the parent as well as the child has a chance to learn and to improve his opinions and actions, to profit from the fact that his child is freely providing him with "feedback" from his behavior and not merely with blind obedience or disobedience.

It is also important that the child be able to speak and act freely with the parent in order to correct himself, his attitudes, inadequate or wrong information, or his insensitivity to some factors involved in his decisions.

So the relationship between parent and child profits greatly both ways from being correctable through feedback both ways. This requires not only that communication be active and open, but that it be encouraged and reinforced by the receptivity and openmindedness of both parents and children to one another.

CHAPTER III

Problems in Discipline

DIFFERENT KINDS OF problems in discipline arise at different ages—even though the basic themes remain the same. Is discipline a matter simply of learning to obey? Do we have to understand the earliest source of each problem as it arises before it can be handled? Does each kind of problem require a different kind of handling? Do different children need different kinds of training? When is a problem important enough to call for special attention and when should it be overlooked? These are some of the questions to be discussed in this chapter.

What Constitutes a Problem?

Problems of various sorts constantly arise in the lives of us all. Each requires some kind of decision, even if the choice is to try to ignore it. Should we go to this movie or that one, or stay home? Should we apply for a job transfer? Should we bathe today or tomorrow? Should we marry this person or that, or neither? Some decisions are obviously much more important than others. Sometimes finding a solution does not matter much to us. Occasionally, among the hundreds of problems we take care of each day without even noticing most, we encounter one which gives us concern, which has some special importance to our future, which marks a point where we can move forward in and enlarge our life or remain rooted to our place, or fall back.

The far-ranging problems of discipline can be similarly classified. Ideally, in disciplining and training children in self-discipline you, as a parent, should try to control and solve *all* problems as they arise. It is most effective for learning to permit no bad habits to develop, no instances of poor learning, contradictory to the desired goals. Thus *each* time a child is allowed to avoid responsibility, to dodge the natural consequences of his mistakes, to ignore stated requirements, to gain a reward without earning it—each such instance retards, however slightly, the development of self-discipline and other skills that will give him his best chance to reach his goals.

Ideally, then, all problems of discipline should be observed and solved as they arise. Practically, however, this is not possible. The active child is doing too much, constantly, to be subject continuously to effective supervision. Besides, the tensions of continuous intervention would distract from the important purposes of living. So parents must single out for attention the most important kinds of behavior they can readily observe. Convenience alone, however, should not be the basis for the parent's intervention. This can happen all too easily. The parent can easily observe long hair and demand that it be cut, or criticize and try to correct a loud voice or a messy room—meanwhile letting the child steal money or toys from his brother because he is not seen doing it.

There should be some consideration of the relative importance of problems and habits in a scale of values, and in reference to the child's future. Honesty should be considered more important than poor grooming, good works be given higher priority than politeness.

For the purpose of this chapter, problems are behavior with which the child has trouble relative to the goals discussed in the last chapter—that is, which are a handicap to the child in trying to reach his goals or, in his immaturity, his guardian's most important goals for him. For practical purposes, the definition also encompasses the view that the problems must be observable and controllable.

Problems of discipline are our main concern in this book. The most directly handled of these problems are illustrated by the child who frequently breaks rules the parents set to safeguard his health, or the health of others, by running in the street, setting fires, beating others or being beaten up without good cause, or shutting himself away from society and vegetating.

The problem becomes a disciplinary one, of course, only when the parent tries to safeguard the child in these respects. If the parent does not care about these matters, they become of concern to society, which tries to deal with neglectful parents. When the community gets notice of such a state of affairs, a social agency will often intervene on behalf of the child. The parent, or the community in the parent's stead, has the responsibility to set rules of conduct to insure the child's survival psychologically and physically. The parent (normally) then tries to discipline the child to accept the rules. Eventually, the child will incorporate these rules in his behavior until they become more or less automatic, and then be "self-disciplined" in these regards. That is, he will develop this behavior into habits which he no longer has to think about. He can then set about spending his energies on other matters.

In a sense, his development is arrested and remains so as long as he has to be fighting his parents on these survival matters, using up his time and energy in these ways—to run in the street, set fires, get into bad fights senselessly, or vegetate.

For the child who is unhappy because he lacks friends, is afraid to participate in neighborhood games or school athletics, cannot dance, or has "nothing to do," the problems can be placed in a different context, from the standpoint of discipline. The parents' job—the disciplinary problem—in such cases is that of teaching the child to take responsibility for these conditions, to decide what kind of behavior might succeed, and to take action that might solve the problems. The parent would learn how to *move* the child in these ways, and the child would learn the discipline of how to use his capacities to solve problems in the future.

There are, then, disciplinary problems determined by what the child needs to do to *survive,* and those determined by what the child needs in order to *flourish* (to reach his goals). Both are vital for the parent to recognize and learn how to solve, and to teach the child to solve.

Sources of Problems

Just as the variety of problems seems infinite, so does their source. Almost any situation can generate problems, or provide new examples of old ones. But the fact that there is such a variety of problems and sources—and, for that matter, solutions—should not obscure the fact that there are some simple principles that can be applied to bring order into the confusion and permit parents to handle the problems well. You, as a parent, don't have to feel bewildered, confused, and overwhelmed by the mass and variety of such situations. Parents can learn some simple, consistent ways of viewing and handling them.

Does the *source* of the problem make a difference in how it can be solved? Generally, very little, we believe. You can spend a great deal of time trying to determine where you have "gone wrong." There may be *some* use in doing this if you can catch yourself soon after the event and determine how to improve your child's actions in the future. There is no value in doing this long after the event occurs and when it can no longer be corrected. Especially in middle age it seems endemic for parents to beat themselves with a sense of guilt. They go over their child-rearing years berating themselves for not being gentler or kinder with their children. They think that they ruined their children with cruel or tough measures. And they may forever after try to make amends by giving gifts to their children when they are adults, or even to their children's children.

Actually the same reason persists as caused whatever failure occurred in the first place: a lack of good training attitudes and methods. The sense of guilt and attempts at amends through gifts are equally futile in correcting whatever problems exist. Even in middle age, with his children grown, the parent can learn to extend a more helpful hand than through gifts, apologies, and guilt. He can still learn how to be of use in helping himself and his children to solve their problems.

Nor is there usually much good purpose in trying to determine the events outside of yourself that may have caused your child serious harm, retarded his development, made him fearful, caused him to avoid trying to solve his problems—unless, of course, such an analysis generates new efforts for the present and future.

How is it useful to decide that you should not have spanked your child in anger for wetting the bed when he was two, if he is still wetting the bed at five? What if a bully kept hitting him on the way from school when he was seven and he is still afraid, at eight, to walk to school alone? What if you insisted that she practice the piano when she was ten, though she wanted to play the organ, and as soon as you let her quit at thirteen she never touched the piano or showed interest in the organ again?

Each of these situations might have been handled better in the first place. There are highly effective solutions to bed-wetting, which we will discuss later. The bully might have been confronted at the time. And the daughter could probably have been allowed to take organ instead of piano lessons with better results.

If the analysis of the source of the problem had been made in time to change the situation, good. However, if the source of the problem is not seen or handled at or near the time it occurs, there is little value in trying to track it down. Not only is it inefficient to look to the past when plenty of current, more directly controllable causes are still around you if the problem is important, but also you can never be sure that recollections of the past are accurate. If you did, for some research study, need accurate information about the past, you would never be contented to discover only what the people involved thought. You would always try to consult more objective sources of information, such as outside observers of the scene.

Why, indeed, look to the past for causes? Suppose a parent was unduly harsh in spanking the child of two for wetting the bed. What can be done about that at age five if the child is still wetting? Can the parent make up for harshness by giving the child extra affection or more toys? Of course not. Giving love or toys to the bed wetter at five, and not attacking the problem of bed-wetting as you would for *any* five-year old bed wetter, regardless of the possible source, would likely just postpone the cure of the problem.

The same with a divorce, and separation from a parent. If the child becomes very nervous afterwards and cries to keep the remaining parent, say the mother, home every evening, it cures nothing to try to "make it up" to the child for the loss of his father by showering him with extra attention. He will not learn in that way how to let go of his mother. He will have to be trained to overcome the problem much the same way as the child of parents living together who cries to keep both parents home every evening—and there are plenty of such children also.

The point we are making is simply this: parents should

concentrate on the problem at hand, as it exists *now,* without great concern about original sources. What they need to know to solve the problem is at hand in the current situation. Whatever is important from the past will be showing itself now, with regard to present conditions. It is only in the present that problems can be solved. And it is seldom too late to solve them.

Deprived of love in the past, the child can learn how to gain it, reasonably, today. Frightened into giving up prematurely, afraid to try new activities and make mistakes, the child can be guided *now* into taking small new steps that can bring him small rewards, and into discovering that mistakes are not disastrous. In this sense, what matters is the training he is given from now on, not what may have produced the problem in the first place.

Furthermore, the development of a problem is seldom sudden and dramatic. It usually occurs by the slow accumulation, in small increments, of bad habits. In this context also, tracing a source becomes much less useful than analysis of what it is that the child is doing *now* that gets him into trouble, defeats him, makes him unhappy.

In the sense of this latter kind of analysis, you might say that you *are* determining the sources of the problem, but putting them into an on-going way of examining matters rather than an historical one. You are discovering the sources, but in the present situation, where they can be handled—not in the past, where they can no longer be touched.

In this view, you might say that the child cries to keep his mother home not because he was deprived of his father last year and thus made insecure (that concentrates on the past and provides no practical solutions now, even if true), but because when he cries, his mother is worried or guilty and *does* stay home with him—and thus he never learns that when she leaves, she also returns. A trial solution can easily be found for such a current source of trouble. The mother can go out, beginning with short periods and gradually extending them, may bring a little present to him or give him an account of her experiences upon her return, and can teach her son through actual demonstration that he *can* learn to endure and become comfortable with her absences.

Are Problems Outgrown?

Very often parents and their friends and professional advisers (physicians, ministers, teachers) will seek reassurance in facing children's problems in the words, "Oh, they'll outgrow it," or "They're just going through a phase," or "Just give them time, be patient, they'll get over it."

These words are like a magic incantation. They have little to do with the reality and variety of problems. They are an attempt to cast a spell on problems to try to make them go away without considering their severity, current cause, or effect.

Many problems will, of course, be solved or disappear in time (as their immediate cause disappears) or diminish to the point that they do not matter. However, others will remain unsolved, will intensify (as current causes increase), or will grow and become increasingly disruptive and defeating.

Parents need not depend upon magic words to provide comfort, meanwhile doing nothing to solve problems. There is a far more reasonable approach: to consider the problem and to make as good an estimate as possible of what is likely to happen with the passing of time. If it looks as if the immediate cause will vanish—as from moving out of a neighborhood or having the residuals of an illness or injury pass, or if the trauma of starting school or the spurt of adolescent growth is the cause and a few months or even a year or two will certainly bring substantial changes automatically—then, of course, one can wait with expectation that the problem will solve itself.

Even so, the parent need not sit idly by waiting for a

problem to go away. The parent may intervene only mildly in some circumstances rather than sharply, but he can always help the problem-solving process. Even when the problem seems to be temporary and likely to be "outgrown," as in starting school, the parent can help the child to master the situation more easily. There is seldom good reason to abdicate the role of guidance and training when *any* problem appears, even when it is likely, eventually, to be solved without parental help. What harm can there be in contributing to a solution?

When you are told, then, that a problem will likely be "outgrown," you can assume this advice has only the value of comforting you when you are feeling helpless and worried. Some problems, of course, are inevitable, and some do come at certain ages. But whether you do nothing about a problem and simply try to wait it out should be decided by the nature and effect of the problem, and not by your sense of helplessness about solving it. If a problem is serious, you should almost always be able to help with it. Even if most adolescents are likely to be somewhat concerned about—and "outgrow" concern about—the onset of adolescence or masturbation, for example, it seems obvious that the parent can ease the child's way into the period and out of the problems. Similarly, no serious problem is likely to be inaccessible to the parent's aid, or to profit from neglect.

The Child's Initiative

Does a continuous training role by the parent weaken the child's initiative? Should not the child be left alone to find his own way as much as possible? Does he not gain independence and skill in handling himself by acting on his own, making his mistakes, and learning from experience?

This attitude recalls a "survival of the fittest" philosophy. Children should not be raised in a germ-free—or problem-free—environment, even if parents were able to provide such. But neither can the parent let the child wander as he will without exposing him to severe physical and psychological damage.

Children do grow up schizophrenic, neurotic, miserable, depressed, unfulfilled, feeling as if they have wasted their lives, blaming others for their troubles, and so on and on through a list of crippling deficiencies. Do parents contribute to these problems by errors of omission or commission? Have they done too little or too much? Do children grow up best left alone to make their own choices and mistakes?

We propose that there is no such thing as too much training, education, teaching—*provided that it is properly directed and applied.* Just as there is no limit to such other good qualities as knowledge, wisdom, skill in crafts, love, neither is there to good parental guidance designed to help children to reach desirable goals.

But our focus must always be on the goals and how we are succeeding with them. As long as we give all of our attention to them, watch to see whether our efforts are helping the child to reach them, and make continuous adjustments according to results, we can always be of help.

If our efforts are producing dependency in the child, then they are misdirected. But providing help need not produce dependency. All of us consult physicians, lawyers, teachers, or other professionals when we have problems. We use their expert help, and neither they nor we usually consider or treat it as a dependency relationship. Sometimes dependency does develop, because either the expert or the client mishandles the situation. But it does not have to develop that way.

We consult an expert and use his help as we see fit. We consider his help as we might consider a tool to help us to build a piece of furniture or to repair an appliance. The expert—or teacher—can provide the tool (in the form of facts or advice, for example) that permits us to solve a problem we have.

He may, of course, take over and actually solve our

problem for us. Some experts do this, are asked to do this. But the ultimate control of their service, its choice and application, rests with the consumer and his exercise of power in the relationship.

Thus we maintain that it is not the fact that professional help is sought and used that determines whether one is showing dependency, but rather how it is used. It can be used to increase independence by making one better informed and more capable in handling one's life.

The parent-child situation need not increase dependency in the child when the parent takes his proper, powerful, and necessary role as teacher and trainer. If one of the goals is to train the child for independence, then that kind of guidance is built into the relationship along with whatever other goals are desired.

Independence is not necessarily fostered by a hands-off policy. Children of all ages can drift helplessly in an entirely permissive atmosphere, and, as a consequence, come to feel more helpless, passive, and dependent than those who receive expert help in achieving their goals of character and personal accomplishment.

How the goal of effective independence can best be reached is, after all, the theme of this book. It is a paradox that for all us human beings successful maturity and independence seem best achieved through reasonable help at crucial times in our lives rather than none—help which permits us to meet challenges, to overcome obstacles, and to gain strength through learning how to succeed in our purposes.

This is what we would seek to provide the child through the skillful intervention of his parents.

CHAPTER IV

Principles of Effective Training

ONE MIGHT SAY that the peak goal of education is self-control, and that all others build to or derive from it. Socrates' admonition to "know thyself" as the highest good, and the "self-realization" or "self-actualization" of many psychologists today, are synonymous with self-control. They all have the same use for us here once we break them down to refer to actual events in one's life.

If we are to gain self-control, self-direction, and related virtues, we need to know how to train (educate) one for these aims. It is one thing to point to a fulfilled man and say he is an effective or an educated person or even to point to many of the rest of us and see where we fail to reach a stellar height in self-development. *How to train* for self-control and self-direction, however, becomes a pressing and challenging problem.

Setting Goals

People do not develop themselves in random or accidental ways. It is true that random and accidental forces operate in all our lives, but the person with reasonable targets in mind will find his way through the chance occurrences better than one without guidance. Setting goals is important, for it not only tells us where we are going, but also helps in setting the means to the goals and in deciding how and when we have arrived at them. In addition, it helps us learn how to set alternate goals if the ones we originally set have to be modified.

Setting goals should be a specific task. We do not simply teach the child to read; we teach him specific reading skills (silent or oral, or both) necessary to perform certain tasks (such as getting through a given reader, being able to read the daily newspaper, following directions for getting around in a city). Just saying we are teaching a child "to read" is much too vague—we must say *what* he is to read and with *what level* of competence and to *what end*.

Often we set goals without specifying fully what we mean, although we know more concretely what we mean. For example, we teach a child to "ride a bike," but we don't mean in order to ride the bike in a six-day bike race, or to thread it through heavy traffic in a big city. We usually mean to ride a bike in his neighborhood, to avoid falling off dangerously, to use judgment so as not to run into others and so as to avoid hazards.

Even though we set goals without specifying the details, we can set the details if we have to do so. A child learns to speak (to some extent) early in his life, but he keeps on refining this speech until he becomes senescent. Is there any point in one's life when he can say he has learned to speak? Yes and no. It depends upon what our goals are. If the child is a bad stutterer, we would probably adopt the goal of moving him toward fluent speech at the vocabulary and sentence structure levels commensurate with his age and intellectual ability. We would probably not expect to make him into a Demosthenes or a successful salesman.

Parents often have vague goals in mind when they wish to bring about some improvement in their child. The first thing some behavior therapists do when parents ask them for help to improve the achievement of a child is to ask them to set down specific goals for behavior change. One such parent said of his fourteen-year-old, eighth-grade boy:

> *Well, we came to see you about John, who is not doing much in school, although he is very smart according to tests—here is his profile of achievement and ability taken just last fall. [Implied goal here is: We wish John to be able to achieve at a higher level.]*

Now it is necessary to look into John's situation to see what, in fact, we may be able to set in the way of educational goals. We know that he is bright—the tests say so, and they are reliable in this respect (they may show him to be lower than he really is, owing to the poor test-taking and reading skills, but they are extremely unlikely to rate him higher than he really is)—and we begin to build on this fact.

If John is not achieving at a level commensurate with his measured ability, we have to look for some reasons. We continue the interview (reported here much abbreviated) with his parents. The psychologist asks John's parents such questions as how John performs on classroom tests, how he studies (that is, his study skills and practices), how he spends his time.

> *Well, you know John does not do well on school tests; he doesn't study much for them and he seems to think he knows the material when he really doesn't. We try to go over some tests—when we know about them—with him and it is easy to see he reads carelessly, does not make notes of important matters, and does not get ready for up-coming tests. He just slides into them. Then, when he gets a low grade, he feels dejected and says, "What's the use, I can't get that darn stuff. . . ." [Implied goal: John needs to learn how*

to study better and to set a study schedule—*times for play, time for studying, and so forth.]*

Later the parents were asked about John's leisure time, his hobbies, what he likes to do just for fun.

> *Oh, he has many hobbies—stamps, coins, model building, and he collects articles and magazines on old trains and trolleys. He does a lot of these things alone, though, which bothers us, too. He's always busy but usually alone. Yet he seems to be liked at school—he was elected vice-president of his class last year. [Implied goal: John is active in things that are educational but* he needs to spend more time on his school work in proportion to his recreational activities. *How can we use the hobbies more effectively to aid John in getting his schoolwork done without destroying his hobbies?]*

This discussion may be two-pronged: It may imply a goal of socializing John more, getting him into more social hobbies, or relating his already proven hobbies to clubs that meet to discuss their mutual interests. For the time being, however, we can let this last implied goal ride until we are dealing more effectively with John's study practices. John is certainly busy; he wastes very little time, and this is all to the good in reshaping his behavior in the desired direction.

In summary, we can say that thus far in the interview with John's parents we have set three (implied) goals:

1. *To improve John's scholastic achievement.*
2. *To teach John better study skills and help him to set an overall study schedule.*
3. *To check out his hobby time and relate it more directly and positively to his schoolwork.*

It took about half an hour with John's parents to set these goals. The rest of the interview time was spent in discussing various related items and in deciding that some problems should not be worked on just now (e.g., fighting with his sister when she teased him, not writing thank-you notes for Christmas and birthday presents). We cannot ride off in all directions and change everything at once. Priorities must be set.

We are not trying to change John in just random or capricious ways. Concrete objectives must be chosen according to certain standards. We need to make them highly specific. How?

Setting Highly Specific Goals

Goals need to be broken down into concrete sub-parts. For example, Goal 1 was to improve John's scholastic achievement. This is too broad for action. How can it be made more specific? First, which subjects need improvement the most? In John's case they are math and science. He needed to take more care in his detailed work, in checking his work, in actually doing his homework assignments *daily*. This led to the following specific set of goals in the form of a *daily schedule,* as follows:

P.M.

3:30-4:00: *Change clothes; get snack; make ten-minute phone calls.*

4:00-4:30: *Do math homework; check work with mother (she was a college math major).*

4:30-5:00: *Correct and finish math work; recheck.*

5:00-5:30: *Read science chapter and answer three (daily assigned) questions.*

5:30-5:45: *Check science work with father (he arrives home at about 5:15 daily).*

5:45-6:15: *Work on stamp or coin hobbies, if above work is in order; if not, continue to correct math or science.*

6:15-7:00: *Dinner time. Help clear the table after dinner.*

7:00-7:30: Read the paper; check for "Current Events" assignments in social studies course; check this work with parents.

7:30-8:30: Do assignments in social studies or English; check with parents on completion of work.

8:30-9:00: Watch favorite TV program, contingent on above-cited work being completed.

9:00-9:45: Bathe, prepare for bed, ready clothes for next day, etc.

John's scheduling is elastic. It depends upon the imminence of exams, on how well he has been concentrating on his work for the past few days, on whether he has much or little homeowrk. The schedule is a *guideline*, not a rigid format. As John moves ahead in his scholastic work and begins to achieve on a level closer to his ability and interest, the schedule can be relaxed even more—but not until he shows clear evidence of solid achievement as judged by his teachers over a substantial period of time. Just one good grade is not enough.

To make his schedule even more attuned to the overall objective of improving his scholastic work, John may need to show his parents an English theme he has written; he may be required to work out sample math problems in preparation for a test; he may have to write up an experiment done at school for a review before handing it in. The details must be secured. Little goals, the "nitty-gritty" of schoolwork, must somehow be set and included in the schedule, developed according to John's strengths and weaknesses and school requirements.

One may note that the second goal set earlier—to teach John better study skills and to make a schedule—has already been included. One goal melds into another; a plan for one purpose tends to meet the demands of several goals. Or one could say that the three goals previously described actually overlap and perhaps some of them are subordinate to others—the schedule may be the high-priority goal, because within its confines the other goals can be accomplished.

The third goal, for example—relating hobbies and school requirements in an efficient manner—may be greatly facilitated by the schedule. One can see to it that hobby activity is built into the schedule, *contingent* upon his progress in schoolwork prior to the assigned recreational time. With proper scheduling, then, all the goals set in this first interview could be actively and gainfully pursued.

Lest this program appear too simple to meet the problems, we should note that it is one matter to make out a schedule on paper and another matter to carry it out successfully. There may need to be a lot of *following through*—attention to detail, support, reinforcement. John may contest the procedures, he may continue to try to get by with careless or incomplete work, or he may go on a kind of "sitdown strike," calling his parents "unfair" or "mean." Whatever form these protests may take, the parents have to feel that they are pursuing a worthwhile course to try to get John back into more even and more productive ways with his schoolwork. They are not treating him wrongly or unfairly. They are simply trying to correct a problem that has been allowed to go on and on in a deteriorating way, making for much emotion and friction and, in a sense, training John in poor work and achievement habits.

Let us summarize what has been said about correcting John's work, and try to make more explicit any implicit principles followed:

1. **Set goals.** *This has been outlined in both broad and specific ways. They were derived from the statement of the problems—John's poor achievement and deteriorating attitudes.*

2. **Plan a schedule.** *A schedule was devised which*

blocked out time not only for schoolwork but for the cherished hobby activities. These activities were encouraged, but used as the basis of a contingency for the schoolwork; "You may work on your stamps (or whatever) when you have satisfactorily completed your schoolwork."

3. Work in specific, small steps. *Sweeping changes are unlikely. They would probably be disruptive, even if they could be achieved. Small steps give the child confidence that he can do well what is required of him; they give the parent confidence in the program and its benefits; and they allow for early feedback from the school when John has begun to improve.*

4. Help develop an individual rate of work. *John was not required to get an A on every test, or to make up all the back work on one weekend, or to meet some other, for him unrealistic objective. Through the schedule, a daily work rate, commensurate with John's needs and abilities, was put in operation. He will not remedy his deficiencies overnight—it may take weeks or months, depending upon how much he is in arrears—but he will be overcoming them gradually while at the same time he is building more successful work habits.*

5. Be prepared to follow through to any necessary extent. *While follow-through is inherent in each of the above steps, the parent must be set to continue his efforts until success is achieved.*

This story about John is a true one. His schoolwork did improve decidedly in about three months' time. Two grading periods of six weeks each, with report cards, reflected the following gains for John:

	Prior Report (before therapy)	First Subsequent Report (6 wks)	Second Subsequent Report (6 wks)
English	C—	B—	B
Math	F	C—	C+
Science	F	D+	B—
Social Studies	D	C	C+
Physical Educ.	C	C	C+
Art/Music	C	C—	C+

Some added benefits accrued, as well, which were a kind of bonus for John and his family. He felt better about his schoolwork—was less discouraged and "dragged out," as he put it—and so his interest in his hobbies improved, too. He was elected president of his stamp collecting group, and was put on a committee with three other youths to represent his school in a city-wide conference during a weekend showing of various hobbies in the junior high schools of the metropolitan area. These social behavior changes impressed and pleased his parents greatly, and they saw the wisdom of trying, through priorities and the use of contingencies and schedules, to improve basic, objective requirements first (the schoolwork), with the benefits derived then radiating or generalizing to other areas such as social behavior.

Are principles of effective training applied? Yes. We are using the momentum of John's hobby interests, the ability of the parents to set a structure within which times are scheduled for work and play, and the inherent value (reinforcement, encouragement) of getting one's work done in an acceptable way.

Interrupting Bad Habits—Instituting Good Ones

One can think of many more serious or disruptive problems than those discussed above in regard to John. What if he had a large number of "bad" habits—cursing his parents, running away from home, cutting school repeatedly, constantly fighting at school? The number of seriously disturbing acts a youngster can perform are legion.

One youngster presented this broad range of disruptive behaviors. His mother described them in this way:

> Ralph is in the sixth grade, you know; but he should be in the eighth grade—he is almost 15. He's flunked twice in the last three years. He won't go to school—that is, regularly. Ummm . . . he just starts off as if he were going, then the school calls me about ten a.m. to ask if he is home sick . . . and I know he is off somewhere. He called us once from a highway phone halfway to Baltimore when he was cold and wet and had only a few cents. He had run away because we didn't let him stay overnight at a friend's house the evening before. We just couldn't . . . he had been so bad we couldn't let him go over there . . . do you think we were wrong about that? He's so sensitive and easily hurt, and he wants his way all the time. . . .

This set of problems seems at first glance to be overwhelming. It appeared that Ralph had very little going for him, and the parents felt hopeless.

It is important for one who is going to help another overcome problems to identify what is "good" or "positive" or "strong" in the troubled one's behavior. What is there about Ralph that will give us a hold to him in some important way? Parents need to provide this information. All the negative and perplexing matters seem to make him inaccessible to help. This is not true, but we must be specific in our attempts to find some positive entrées into Ralph's behavioral economy. The following response to the question "What does Ralph like to do that is good or positive?" occurred in a conversation with the parents:

> *You ask what does he like that is allowable, that is good or positive? That's a ringer . . . for Ralph, anyhow. . . . Maybe I could answer that for my other children easier. Uhmmmm. [Thinks for a few minutes] . . . Well, he was in a class play last spring and he was superb! The dramatics teacher said he was a "natural," but she couldn't get him to come to rehearsals regularly—he just squeaked by, but he ad-libbed so well he was a scream! And funny, too!*

Some discussion revolved around his theatrical talents, and it was felt that this was too occasional an area of activity for Ralph right now to serve any immediately useful purpose—though it might in later years. What else did he have going for him?

> *He likes small children—someone said they made him feel important—and he can teach them things with the utmost patience. Here again, he's acting in a sort of way, holding someone's attention, getting attention glued on him. Hmmmmm . . . that may be worth pursuing; we have lots of kids in our neighborhood who need "sitters."*

This was elaborated on further, a small group of neighborhood children was invited over each Saturday morning for a few hours to be entertained and schooled by Ralph in the family basement, where his mother was available if needed and where some supervisory control could be exercised. If Ralph was paid for this work, all the better. It might mean that he would get his "lesson" for the children ready on Friday evenings, as well as earning money and gaining a sense of achievement.

This plan worked very well; Ralph even contacted the parents of neighborhood children and developed a clientele. He talked with the teachers about his lessons for the children; this was tied in with his own work at school under the teachers' supervision. The only problem was whether Ralph would keep up the responsibility over a sustained period of time. It was partly the problem faced by the parents and the therapist in working out the contingencies so that this hold to Ralph could be pivoted widely enough to get him back on a more even keel in his own schoolwork and in his relationships at home. To help gain the latter purposes, Ralph's mother agreed to serve Ralph and his students their choice of cookies and drinks at the end of the Saturday morning session. At first the mother was going to serve the refreshments at the beginning of the school day, but acquainting her with the use of contingency management methods allowed her to use her own good will and effort in a way reinforcing to the children involved.

The program outlined above began promptly after Ralph got his clientele. There were some rocky sessions, with children leaving or clamoring for their own preferences in play activities over Ralph's efforts to lead them, but gradually, with Ralph's mother stepping in now and then to quiet and restructure their activities, they achieved an even keel for several months. This steady time enabled Ralph to gain some good experiences in self-control insofar as *his* schoolwork and general attitudes were concerned, and it benefited the youngsters in the neighborhood. Ralph's mother commented on how the whole program progressed from early spring to the end of school, a total of about three and one-half months:

> *If you had told me this about Ralph, I would never have believed it. Seeing is believing! He became a different kid in the three months. Now he's working in a summer camp as a group leader of*

children six to ten years old. Oh, I don't mean that we didn't have our ups-and-downs—we certainly did—and there were times when I just knew the whole Saturday school, as he called it, would fold or, even worse, come crashing through the kitchen floor from the basement. He had, usually, eight to ten children there, you know. And he pored over books about play activities, games, party games, and everything he could think of. He tried too hard most of the time . . . but then he learned a lot.

During the spring when Ralph ran his "Saturday school" he did improve some in his schoolwork, but not enough, the parents felt. However, Ralph was gainfully occupied with his school and he did not cause as much trouble at home or at school as heretofore. He was asked by two of his regular teachers at his elementary school to give a report in social studies class on his Saturday school. He even got some volunteers from his classmates to help him run the school. However, this particular plan did not work out well. Ralph wanted to run *his* Saturday school, and his proprietary attitude—while good in many respects—turned off some of his peers who had hoped to be included in this (to them) exciting work.

It was another year before Ralph did his regular schoolwork seriously, when he entered junior high school and had several teachers he liked very much.

In summary, what were the goals set for Ralph to cope with his problems at home and school?

The first goal was to *improve his regular schoolwork.* Some progress was made. He got work done more often on a daily basis, and there was therefore less conflict with his parents about his free time at home.

This goal was implemented through a daily schedule which took into account the requirements for each school subject and followed about the same timing as that described earlier for John. That is, there were half-hour study times, breaks, check-outs with parents, reports from school as to how his work was progressing. His grades for the two final six-week grading periods, concurrent with running his Saturday school, were:

	Fourth 6 Weeks (prior to therapy)	Fifth 6 Weeks	Final 6 Weeks
English	F	D	D+
Social Studies	D	C—	C
Math	F	D	C—
Science	D—	D	C
Art/Music	C	C	C+

The following year, Ralph raised his grades further. There were "no disciplinary encounters," as the principal expressed it, during his entire seventh-grade year, and no days when he played "hooky."

A second major goal was to *improve Ralph's attitude toward and handling of his parents.* His interest in his Saturday school was quite powerful at first, although it waned a little bit, as one might expect, as the weeks wore on and when he had trouble disciplining the children. These were good talking points, however, with his parents, and they were able to relate the troubles Ralph had with *his* students to the problems the parents had experienced with Ralph. This was an eye-opening comparison to Ralph, the parents felt.

In achieving this goal, the contingencies were used that allowed Ralph to prepare for his Saturday school by going to the library in the evening two days each week, after he had done his daily assignments for his regular classwork. Daily reports from his teachers, and later weekly reports, kept Ralph's parents constantly informed as to his progress at school. In turn, Ralph was saving for a desk for his own room, which he had picked out and had made a deposit on at a local store, using money raised from his Saturday school "tuition." Each week he banked these dollars toward the desk, and this helped to keep him well motivated toward his Saturday school—which, in turn, helped to tie him in effectively with his own daily work. These two contingency arrangements were powerfully effective not only in ending his wasteful and antagonistic behavior, but also in bringing about his more constructive work in his own school and in his regular elementary school classes.

A third goal, which was a kind of bonus and originally not planned for, was Ralph's opportunity to *build additional goals upon early successes*, by working in a local summer camp teaching youngsters similar to those in his Saturday school, for a ten-week period. The camp also afforded him an opportunity to play on a ball team with his peers at the camp, to learn lifesaving (he was already a pretty good swimmer), and to see two or three professional ball games on Sundays during the end of the summer camp season. This turn of events came when Ralph's teacher heard about his Saturday school and offered to put him in touch with the camp director, who was a relative of Ralph's teacher. This event shows how fortunate additions can result from early small successes, how successes can become habitual and replace habitual failures built into a vicious circle. Reinforcing opportunities beget reinforcing opportunities; success becomes contagious!

Some Additional Concepts

Certain supportive concepts and practices can fill out the picture here. These include: Work Before Reward; Initial Start (or Kick); Small Steps Leading to Large Gains; Regularity; Immediacy of Feedback (Reinforcement); Consistency (with Firmness and Fairness); and Restitution. These will be discussed in order.

Work Before Reward. This is, of course, the heart of any contingency arrangement: you get your reinforcements (rewards) after and only after you have done the work. If this kind of "discipline" is not followed, how is the child to learn the difference between what is rewardable and what is not, between what is desired and not desired? Some workable distinctions have to be made between what "goes" and what "does not go." If stoplights did not clearly indicate red for STOP and green for GO, learning to produce safe, effective regulation of traffic could not result.

There are more reasons than just orderliness, however, for the Work Before Reward paradigm. There is the satisfaction that one *can* accomplish something; that things and people can be managed successfully; that goals can be reached. Miserable people often despair of ever having an accord with themselves, with nature, with others—everything is, to them, unreliable and unpredictable. They lack satisfaction in what they try to do because in their minds there is no clear separation of fact from fantasy, no separation of that-which-works from that-which-doesn't-work. One gains confidence, on the other hand, upon learning (getting feedback, being reinforced) that he is able to *do something.* The reinforcement at the end of the line tells one that he is operating well; his work earns a payoff.

Initial Start (or Kick). Progress has to start somewhere, usually gradually and in smaller ways than we wish. A beachhead must be obtained and followed up.

In the case of John and of Ralph, described above, there was always a deliberate and painstaking effort to get a foothold, to begin in any reasonable way available, even though there was no assurance that all would go well. Without these small starts—these "initial kicks"—with John and Ralph, there would have been no progress. Successes come mostly to those who make attempts to solve problems. The small start provides feedback, or reinforcement, and the confidence that there is some successful or hopeful movement. The small start and the feedback information (encouragement, reinforcement, reward) that results, provide the basic information needed to change the course of events, to solve problems, to build confidence in problem-solving skills and, most important, in oneself.

A small start, like a slight push on an immense boulder on a slope, can produce accelerating and large results indeed.

Small Steps Leading to Large Gains. Many professionals as well as parents expect too much too soon of children. Exorbitant expectations, when unfulfilled, as by definition they usually are, produce negative feedback that discourages the child and anyone involved in the program of change. Too often schools have said to the student who has "flunked out" or been put on probation: "When you come back you must make A's or B's to overcome these D's and F's." The depleted and poorly trained student cannot jump from failure to resounding success—he needs time, gradual steps, successive approximations, and good feedback from his early efforts. Restoration is a gradual process; it seldom occurs in one giant step. Failure to recognize this makes recouping less probable than it could be and may turn chances for success into additional failure.

Some of the most important innovations in education in the last decade, in connection with programmed instruction, learning with the aid of computers, and other better-structured ways of presenting materials, are based upon the relevance, even necessity, of small steps. Big problems seem best solved by breaking them down into smaller problems and working on them gradually.

Regularity. Regularity has the effect of cementing change, of building a bulwark against capriciousness in effort and unreliability of change. Other conditions being equal, a child who has no systematic set of "do's" and "don't's" from his parents and teachers is probably not as able to progress toward his goals as the one who knows where he stands, what standards he should apply.

The absence of regularity tends to produce emotional problems. Think how each of us would feel if confronted day after day, or even intermittently, with unpredictable attitudes on the part of a boss, if the car would not start reliably, if the route to work changed each day, if the pay checks were never for a predictable amount, if the attitudes of friends could not be counted on! Regularity provides for order and dependability in the child's life; the absence of it produces disorder and frustration and curtails productivity and satisfaction.

Many parents do not handle their children consistently. The parent or teacher will say, in perplexity, "Well, I've tried *everything.*" This emphasis on "everything" is supposed to indicate willingness to change and be flexible, but from the standpoint of getting reliable change or growth from the child, it often appears as inconsistency. It usually means the child is confronted with a myriad of demands and counter-demands, changes and contradictions. Parents (and teachers) will say they have tried "being harsh," "being easy," "paying no attention," and so on, as if they treat the child like a lock to which they are trying to find a key from a ring full of keys. In fact, adults often use the expression, "Trying to find a key to his thinking," in this very context.

Regularity, even when its direction is perhaps not highly desirable, is probably much better than constant aimless change. The parent who gets angry and admonishes—realizing that positive methods are much better—is at least more consistent that the parent who changes in exasperation and throws up his hands in hopelessness. Many children have emerged strong from regularly "bad" homes—they have learned to live with, to get around, to find a way in spite of, inconsiderate and punitive parents.

This is no justification for such difficult homes, but even a steadily harsh discipline is probably less damaging than one that is alternately and inconsistently harsh, soft, noncommittal, or neglectful.

While regularity is the hallmark of stability in dealing with the child, educationally and emotionally, it should be tied to fairness and firmness.

Consistency (with Firmness and Fairness) is to permit the child to be regulated and educated by a dependable stance on the adult's part, though with as much acceptance and cooperation as possible. Adding firmness and fairness to consistency enables the child more easily to accept constraints, to take disappointments, and to handle his own problems emotionally in the context of a dependable adult world that has his welfare at heart. The child's interest should be solicited so that when he is not angry or disappointed he can recognize that he feels more secure and confident with firm parental or teacher handling.

Restitution. This is a training device to be used when the teacher or parent cannot take preventive action but must act after the deed. A child breaks the toy of another child; a student in school makes off with the pen of his neighbor in the classroom; a group of boys carelessly break a window near where they are playing ball; a careless child throws soft-drink bottles into a driveway where cars go and where children sometimes play. Such transgressions call for some kind of after-the-fact correction. How can restitution be carried on in a constructive way, in a way that avoids punitiveness for its own sake, and unnecessary emotional entanglements, but has an impact upon future behavior and helps to train the child?

The child should, of course, be warned by parent or teacher that, as a general policy, he will have to make up for any careless destructive act. The parent can set the style for this viewpoint in small ways—by having the child with dirty shoes go back outside the house and clean his shoes, as well as clean up the mess he has made by coming in untidy in the first place. The wise parent will not stop with the statement "Haven't I told you before about coming into the kitchen with muddy shoes? Now you just go to your room while I have to rescrub and repolish the floor." Such a statement can, in fact, do harm. Why? In the first place, it makes the child feel guilty for his carelessness. It does not, in the second place, get the dirt and mud cleaned up. And a third error and unnecessary complication is fostered by the parent's attitude of martyrdom, which is likely to smoulder while she cleans the floor and at the same time despairs of having the child learn the correct behavior.

Children will come into the house dirty and they will act in ways inconsiderate of adults. If one starts with the fact that the child will do such things, one can move to the view that he has to be taught to do otherwise, and not merely punished. The problem is to get the child to establish good habits with regard to entering the house. If the child comes in with muddy feet he can be made to go back out again; he can be told to clean his shoes outside; he can then be made to clean up the mud he just left on the floor.

Very simple? Yes! Most problems can be solved in simple ways, if these ways are thought out as described in this chapter, and if they are carried out patiently and in reasonable ways.

CHAPTER V

Using Nonprofessional and Professional Help

WHEN IS A child's problem serious enough to require professional help? When should a parent give up on trying to help the child and turn to an expert? When is the child's problem to be called "special," not likely to be outgrown or solvable by the resources of the child and his parents?

The same questions are raised about adult problems, and the same answers apply. When do *you* seek professional help for *yourself?* How do you decide when you cannot solve *your* problems and need to turn to an expert? And not only personal problems. The same kind of questions arise in connection with medical and legal and religious problems. When is it wise for you to turn to others for help?

For a detailed description of how to decide on the need for help, types of help available, where to obtain it, how much to pay, and other questions lightly touched on in this chapter, you can consult the book *A Practical Guide to Psychotherapy*, by Dr. Wiener (Harper & Row, 1969).

Nonprofessional Help

Interacting with people around you, particularly those

you are close to, is more likely than perhaps any other method to generate new approaches to and ways of solving your problems—better, probably, than reading, listening to lectures, thinking entirely by yourself, or getting professional help.

Many people interact so frequently and extensively with others that it is habitual for them to be eliciting suggestions, opinions, and advice directly or indirectly at all times that they are not giving it. Getting feedback continuously this way for their ways of thinking and acting, and gaining new perspectives and suggestions on problems in their life they are, if reasonably open-minded and attentive, able to draw upon a variety of sources for solutions to their difficulties.

The ability to find congenial and helpful friends and acquaintances, and to use critically the help available from conversations with them, is usually what distinguishes successful parents from unsuccessful parents—not necessarily the ability to handle all child-rearing problems themselves. They may learn a great deal through experience or through the example of how their parents raised them. But to use their knowledge and experience best, they need also to test it out, refine and adjust it in conversations with others. Otherwise they are likely to get off into at least some rigid, unsuccessful, or inefficient ways without realizing it. Anyone who is not exposed to feedback and correction from others in his life who are candid and knowledgeable seems likely to develop some peculiarities that curtail his effectiveness.

The variety of sources of nonprofessional help is almost as great as the variety of human beings. Almost anyone of any status can, at crucial times, be of great help in vital ways. What *you* bring to the situation and how you use the proffered aid is perhaps as important as what the other person suggests. The nonprofessional may simply listen or draw you out, and you provide your own solutions by putting into words some vague thoughts you have had. Or he may, by some offhand comment, provide you with an idea or perspective that triggers answers for you. Even a child or stranger may accidentally serve this purpose.

But there are better and poorer ways to find a nonprofessional who can help you—just as there are wiser and less wise ways to find a professional to aid you. A close friend can be sought out to talk to on the basis of his general intelligence or wisdom, or simply because he or she seems to have done a good job with marriage or child-rearing or handling money or a death—whatever is your problem. A certain teacher may seem to be a good adviser on a bullying child because you know she has handled some in her class very well, a particular minister may seem good for a boy using drugs because he has close touch with a youth group, a social worker who belongs to your precinct organization and has marched with kids in support of mutual aims may seem to have something to offer you with your high-school dropout daughter.

The better informed, the more specific, the more open you can be in choosing and using any source of such help, the more you are likely to get from it. Conversely, blindly seeking out a friend, minister, youth leader, or physician simply because he is available or has high standing in his field or in the community—without information about his knowledge or wisdom in the area of your particular problem—makes it likely you will be disappointed in the advice or suggestions you obtain.

Perhaps the most important benefit you can gain from discussing your problems with a nonprofessional friend or acquaintance is to obtain an objective viewpoint. You describe how your child misbehaves at the dinner table and the friend, teacher, or minister comments that it sounds as if your Bobby is spoiled, and that he needs a firmer hand.

You may reply that you already know this, that your "counselor's" advice is right—but. . . .And you go on to add how you feel sorry for Bobby, being the youngest in the family, or because his father is so hard on him, or how he is so cute or sensitive. You are being affected by factors that are *irrelevant* to training him properly, and any wise nonprofessional can see this in sharper focus, and with less distraction, than you can, because he is not affected by the *causes* as you are, but only by the results and how best to handle them.

Another aid that a nonprofessional adviser or friend can contribute is a sharing of experience. Not only can he help you realize that your problems are common and solvable, but he can add information about what has worked and has not worked in other situations in a way that extends your experiences.

He can also generate new ideas of how to attack your problems, to supplement any ideas you may have. He may be able to exercise some special influence with your child. He may be able to help arrange for concrete aids such as special tutoring, youth groups, playmates, recreational facilities.

There is some research evidence that nonprofessional help can be as good as or better than professional help. This should not surprise us. Professional psychologists or social workers or psychiatrists have no corner on the wisdom of the world, nor on the wise men. There is far more of both available outside any profession than in it. The comments and advice of friends and acquaintances who know you and your child fairly well are likely to be more immediately and concretely relevant and useful than those of professionals, at least before they have taken some weeks to get well acquainted with you. And even then they may not choose to be highly specific in their advice.

You may, of course, get foolish comments or poor suggestions, and you must be able to evaluate them well. But you should do this with professionals also, since they will differ widely among themselves and no two are likely to make the same recommendations or pursue the same course of treatment.

You can lose little and gain much, in any case, by seeking out the wisest friends and acquaintances, evaluating their comments, and judiciously trying out their suggestions. It is really only the practical value of their suggestions that matters—whether what they say helps you to solve your problems with your child. And the results with the child will prove that soon enough.

Thus, although it is efficient to seek out the best kind of nonprofessional help (as well as professional, when that is necessary), you need not be worried about getting poor advice *if* you use your intelligence, sense, and experience to judge it to a reasonable extent before applying it. That is, you should not try it if it appears likely to be shallow, damaging, or biased, though you should also try not to prejudge and eliminate it without a fair trial if it *may* have some value.

Above all, however, you need to be able to judge the results for yourself. If you can judge them yourself, you need not worry about incomplete or miserable results. If this method fails, you will simply have to try another. You must make mistakes and experience failures. If you don't, you are not trying enough new and hopeful approaches, you are not taking enough chances ever to find by the essential screening-out process what works best.

Who Needs Help?

First of all, let us consider *who* needs the help when, finally, professional help is needed—parents or child. This is a vital question which you must be prepared to answer for yourself, since the professionals are sharply split on it. Some psychologists, psychiatrists, social workers, and counselors will see your child one, two, even three or four hours a week, with or without separate interviews with you. Some will insist that you see a different therapist.

Some may see you and your child together, sometimes or always. Some therapists will involve both parents, not just one, and some will bring in the whole family, including all the other children, all in one grand series of family interviews.

There is no generally accepted system to these various combinations, although many therapists will insist vehemently that theirs is the best or only successful method. That is, a typical therapist will not work with all of these different combinations. He will generally follow just one approach for most of his cases. He will see just the child, or just a parent and a child separately, or just the family all together, or just the parent or parents. He has usually decided how he will proceed before he knows the nature of your child's particular problem. He *believes in* "family therapy," or psychoanalytic methods with the child alone, or working just with parents on how to help the child, but there is no good scientific evidence to help you decide which method is best in which situation.

You should know ahead of time, then, how the particular therapists you are considering prefer to handle children's problems, and choose a therapist according to what approach makes the most sense to you.

This means giving serious thought to the matter and trying to discover the arguments for each theory about who should be seen. Here, briefly, are some of the arguments:

Therapy with the child only. *For this view:* The child needs help in handling his feelings and problems. He needs a warm, understanding adult to experience affection towards, to respect and to learn from, to gain strength from to handle his life. His parents have failed in these regards, but the therapist can succeed in building his capacity for a good relationship with adults and a sense of love and support from a parent-like person. And once the child has experienced the good relationship, he is better able to cope with some bad old relationships.

Against this view: The therapist cannot possibly fulfill such grand goals in an hour or two a week. It is difficult to succeed in therapy with an adult, and the child is much less able to learn this way from conversation. If the therapist just talks or even plays with the child, and the child still has to go home and live with incompetent or unfeeling parents, the child can never surmount the obstacles to a good relationship. To return even a restored child to the scene and cause of his troubles is like sending the cured drug addict back to his original circumstances. In the old environment the likelihood of relapse is high, if the conditions have not been changed.

Therapy with the parents only. *For this view:* The parents are always realistically the most powerful influence in the life of the child who lives with them. The child spends most of his waking hours under parental control of some sort, and training the parent in how to handle him well is by far the most efficient and effective way to help the child to overcome his problems. Compare the one, two, or three hours a week the therapist can spend with the child with the ten to twenty waking hours a week the child is likely to be around home and subject to the influence of the parents. For the therapist to train the parent to handle and help the child effectively is a far more efficient use of the therapist's time than trying to change the child's behavior directly.

Against this view: The child needs to experience a warm, loving, competent adult in a way the parents cannot provide. Even if parents try to follow the therapist's suggestions, they are not likely to be as good about it as is necessary. They may even be resentful about taking directions, to the point of added hostility toward the child. Besides, the child needs to feel that he has someone on his side in his conflicts with his parents, that he is sometimes right in his battles and should not feel guilty or upset when he disagrees with them.

Therapy mixed, with parents and child(ren): Therapy which is mixed between parents and child(ren) in various combinations and time arrangements shares all the advantages and disadvantages of both previously discussed approaches. In addition, the major advantage is said by advocates to be that the more members of the family are involved—including the siblings and occasionally other relatives, or even friends, of the child with problems—the more understanding there can be of causes and the more help can be elicited and used to produce change.

The major special disadvantage of this procedure would seem to be the dilution of responsibility and efforts for change. Where the child or parent is clearly the therapist's client, the therapist will presumably try to help that person to take responsibility for making changes occur. The therapist will try to teach his client how to gain some control and direction in his life *regardless* of who might be blamed for his troubles or who else theoretically could bring about change if he wanted to. When various members of a family are being seen, however, no one client is clearly the focus of the change effort, or is taking full responsibility, and no one's effort is therefore as likely to be as intense as when there is only one client.

When Is Help Needed?

There is no sharp line the crossing of which tells you that you need professional help for a problem with your child. There is no special advantage, however, in going to the extreme of not seeking help until the child is so disturbed or ineffectual that everyone involved with him would agree without question that he needs special attention—or of seeking help at the first sign of trouble that the parents cannot handle with their usual methods.

If you wait until he is extremely disturbed and there is no question of the need for professional help, you will have failed to gain that help when it could have been briefer and more limited than has become necessary. Also, chances are you would have waited for poor reasons—embarrassment about admitting that you need help from others, or looking upon professional help as a painful or radical last-resort procedure.

Once you admit your need for help, you will discover that many parents, perhaps most, have also, on occasion, had to seek special help for a child from *someone*—a friend, minister, relative, teacher, youth leader, family agency, or psychological professional. And also your need for help need involve no more than visits to any other technical expert for help—a lawyer for a legal problem, a physician for a medical problem, a contractor for a house drainage problem.

In seeking professional help at the first sign of a problem, you will be overlooking rich sources of aid that are close at hand, in your own knowledge, inventiveness, and experience, and in those of friends, relatives, and other persons whose services are free and voluntary.

There is little lost by trying to utilize any new ideas and methods you or others close at hand can generate before looking for professional help. How to do this efficiently will be discussed in the next section. Nonprofessional help can be just as useful as professional, and if the criteria for its success are clear so that you can tell whether it is working or not, you can in fairly short order obtain, try, and judge it before the need for professional help is established.

The need for help of *some* kind can be decided on three grounds. Many more are possible and will be suggested, but these appear to be the least ambiguous, the most direct, and the most useful in terms of implications for the child's life:

a. Is the child's behavior disorganized or disrupted to the point where he seldom if ever succeeds in what he undertakes or what he is reasonably assigned by parents and teachers?

b. Does the child feel miserable, depressed, or inadequate most of the time, either by his own report over a substantial period of time or by the report of those closest to him? (He may or may not recognize or verbalize his unhappiness—but then he usually does not for happiness either.)

c. Are the child's and parents' efforts to overcome the problems mostly unsuccessful, with little realistic hope that such efforts will soon change radically enough to become successful?

The nub of the above ways to decide when the child needs special help is that he is unsuccessful, unhappy, and with poor prospects for improvement. How much unhappiness, how unsuccessful, and how poor the prospects before aid should be sought is difficult to decide. But there is no reason why the parents ever should not reasonably and moderately intervene to help the child when their help is likely to strengthen the child's own skills and successes.

Parents are overprotective and weaken instead of strengthening the child only when they perform for the child, when they smooth his path with their skills, when they substitute their capabilities for the child's instead of helping the child to develop his own.

The child can always profit from the right kind of help. In this sense, training whose purposes are clearly set and followed cannot be overdone. The parent or any other teacher may need to find a balance between the gains from raw experience and from training, but the child can never have too much help of the kind that strengthens his skills.

When special attention should be sought, however— when parents should be alarmed and go out of their way to provide or seek aid—can be decided partly by the length of time the problem has persisted and partly by the extent of the child's disruption. Withdrawal from friends or deteriorated grades at school might be viewed with concern if it goes on for six months or more, but concern enough to seek causes is probably reasonable at three months. On the other hand, if you can catch the tendency to withdraw from friends because of embarrassment at having been beaten in a fight or caught kissing a friend, or failing to do school work because of fear of the teacher's criticism of poor work, then giving attention to the problem at its onset is even better.

The intensity of the disruption can be viewed similarly. Ideally, any degree of disruption in the child's movement toward worthwhile goals is undesirable and should be avoided. Naturally not all disruption can be avoided. However, when the child has almost continuous violent outbursts of rage, or when he sits staring into space during all of his time out of school, more than a day or two of neglect by parents seems unjustified. There is no good reason to let severe disruption go on at all, provided that parents can think of something possibly useful to do to help the child.

This, really, is the crux of the problem of when help is needed. Rather than look for an answer in terms of the problem, one might do better to look for an answer in terms of whether help is *possible*. There is no sense in letting a problem go on, untouched, for longer than one minute after it has been observed, if something can be done to solve it.

The ultimate purpose of training the child is, ideally, to provide him with the attitudes, skills, and self-discipline necessary to solve his problems as soon as they arise. Whenever he is able to do this, the problem does not last long enough or become conspicuous enough to come to the attention of the parent. But whenever the child cannot handle a problem and fumbles unsuccessfully with various ways of dealing with it, parents (and other teachers of the young) should probably intervene with any ways they can, to teach the child to handle the problem—*not* to handle the problem for the child (unless it is destructively overwhelming or dangerous to his physical or mental health).

Is parental intervention likely to help? Is nonprofessional advice likely to help? Is professional assistance likely to help? In this order, the need for help should be considered and provided whenever the child shows signs of being unable to cope with any important problem in his life.

This book is devoted largely to ways in which parents *can* help their children to develop competence in handling their lives, so we will not discuss the parents' role further here, except for this: The parent should not give up on extending his aid and looking for help from others, until he has creatively considered all possible *new* ways he can approach the child and his problems. Flexibility and creativity are extremely important qualities for any problem-solving, and not merely one's initial reaction and suggestions for attacking a problem. The best parents—as well as the best teachers, counselors, and therapists—are constantly generating, considering, and trying out new ways of solving problems when customary old ways do not work. In this sense, the worst crime on the problem-solving scene is to persist with unsuccessful methods, and then to blame someone or something else for the failure—or oneself for not trying hard enough—when a new approach is almost always possible.

When the parent thinks he has exhausted all of his potential for assisting the child, then it is time enough to turn to friends, relatives, and other nonprofessionals for whatever aid they can extend or suggest.

Choosing Professional Help

Suppose, then, you reach a point in trying to handle a problem with your child where your own help has proved ineffectual, despite various inventive efforts over a period of months, and where the problem is disrupting the child's life and making him feel miserable much of the time. Suppose, further, that you have exhausted all sources of help you can think of among your friends and acquaintances.

You are now confronted with the strong possibility that if you do *not* seek professional help your child will continue to suffer and not only not grow but lose ground because of depression, uncertainty, and feelings of inadequacy based upon truly acting ineffectually. And you have no realistic reason to hope that matters will improve, that he will outgrow his troubles, or that some new events or factors will intervene to resolve the situation.

Now it is logical to seek out the most expert and presumably most powerful source of help—the professional in child behavior change. This expert is most likely to be a psychologist or psychiatrist specializing in problems with children, although he also may be a social worker, counselor, teacher, or any other professional in the field of human behavior who has specialized training and experience in handling problems of the young.

A special condition exists in the field of psychotherapy and counseling that does not arise as acutely in other professional fields and that makes choosing capable help especially difficult. That condition is the secrecy of practices in the field.

In law, medicine, engineering, dentistry, teaching, the methods and results of the practitioner tend to be on public display, or at least open to inspection—if not by the public in some instances, at least by colleagues or examining boards and committees.

In the field of human behavior change, however, secrecy is the rule. Hardly ever is the therapy hour observed, or the results objectively examined or displayed. Nor are even records usually available for inspection of any kind. In the name of confidentiality, the client is entirely at the mercy of the individual practitioner, whose own colleagues can seldom be fully aware of his practices.

Is there a solution to such a situation where the consumer has so little protection? We believe so; it is outlined in detail in an earlier book by D. N. Wiener, *A Practical Guide to Psychotherapy* (Harper & Row, 1969). Let it suffice here merely to note that "confidentiality" does not have to rule out all observation of the practitioner and his methods *if the client is willing* to have an interview observed under special conditions which only somewhat abridge its privacy; and other devices can be utilized to protect the client (consumer), including more public information about practitioners and care by professional boards.

Inferior Bases for Selection

Our earlier comment that no one has a monopoly on wisdom in helping human beings applies to your choice of a professional to help you. Choosing someone who is accredited by state and national boards as a specialist in human behavior (usually social work, psychiatry, or psychology) is merely the crudest kind of screening for competence. It eliminates some excellent people and passes through some grossly ineffective ones—but in general those it passes through are likely to be more competent than those it screens out.

Excellent professionals are much better determined, however, we believe, by information other than professional accreditation. Similarly with public reputation. While it is true that a professional who has practiced in a community for many years will have his gross deficiencies of character and professional activities known, his public reputation for competence is likely to be based considerably upon his charm and public and social presence, which have nothing to do with his professional results. Often there are sharp discrepancies between what the public *believes* about him and what his professional colleagues *know* about him from observing his work or hearing him talk intimately about it.

Another method the public often uses to judge a professional's ability is his public lectures and writing. They can be useful indicators of the practitioner's attitudes and practices, but usually they are too vague to tell you exactly how he goes about his work, or specifically how he is likely to proceed with you. Even in his writings for his colleagues, the professional is likely to comment in such vague terms as "we worked through the problem," or "I interpreted his behavior and he got insight," or "I helped the parents to understand the situation better," without really telling you exactly how he helped to change behavior and what the patient did differently.

You might also try to choose a professional by what his current patients say about him. Of the four bases for selection cited so far, this is perhaps the best source of concrete information of what he is likely to do for you. Yet even this one is inferior to alternative methods to be suggested next. Current patients do not have a complete picture of their own treatment, and their positive or negative comments cannot be founded upon final results, but only upon whether they so far like the practitioner and whether he has produced quick results, which may very well be transitory.

But there are better methods of choosing a good practitioner.

Superior Methods of Selection

Perhaps the best single method of choosing professional

help is the one the professionals use for themselves and their families: inside information from professional colleagues within the field of help you are seeking. No one is likely to have more information about the character, practices, and results of the child behavior specialist than fellow professionals who have worked with him, observed his work firsthand, or observed the results of his work by seeing his former patients.

How can you, a member of the public, obtain such intimate information about him as his colleagues may have? It is extremely difficult, and you probably cannot succeed unless you have a close friend in the profession or close to someone in the profession, who can get such information for you. Colleagues protect each other. Every professional man knows of one or more fellow practitioners who are emotionally disturbed, incompetent, dishonest, perhaps even damaging to clients, but does not report them to professional boards because of sympathy or professional courtesy. Every professional man tends to choose professional services for himself and his family far more carefully than he does for strangers, acquaintances, or even clients. Where he may only consider one or two colleagues for his purposes, he may be willing to name several more to a member of the public.

How close you can get to a competent, sensitive, and sympathetic professional in the field will determine how good the information is you can get about a professional who can help you or your child. And on so important (and expensive) a matter, it will pay to expend considerable effort.

Obtaining a trial interview before deciding on a therapist is also a good way of deciding for yourself whether you are likely to profit from the offered help. You cannot decide wisely, of course, just how successful the help will be, nor should you try to judge the quality of the practitioner by any general comments he makes, or by his charm.

To use a trial session wisely, you should come to it prepared to ask specific questions about how the therapist usually proceeds with your kind of a problem, how he views your (your child's) problem, how long he thinks it will take or what the length will hinge on, how much it will cost and what provisions can be made for payment, what results he has had in previous cases such as yours, and anything else that is relevant to deciding between one therapist and another.

Unfortunately, it is expensive to shop in this way. Each therapist will charge you his ordinary interview fee, which ranges from $15 to $35 (closer to the upper end if you are not poor). Anything you can find out free ahead of time, or without a personal session, is obviously desirable. So whatever the prospective psychotherapist or counselor has done that is in the public domain should be consulted.

While general lectures and writing are often too vague to be useful for your purposes, *if* he has been specific, publicly, on how he helps people, or if you can get him to be specific, you can profit in your selection process. You can try to talk briefly by phone to him or to his secretary with your specific questions. You can ask him questions at any public lectures he may give. You can write him a letter asking for answers to your questions.

Finally, one of the best ways to find out just what he does in his interviews is to talk to clients who have finished treatment with him, more than one or two if possible. They are not easy to find unless you happen to know them as friends or acquaintances who have talked about their treatment. Perhaps, *with the permission of the clients,* therapists should have such a list available for judicious use.

In any case, if you can find informed, objective ex-patients with problems like yours, you should be able to discover exactly how the therapist is likely to proceed with you. Even though any therapist would say that he tends to proceed somewhat differently with each patient, outside observers who have studied the process can observe certain consistencies in his attitude, style, and methods which will be helpful for you to know about, and your only source may be ex-patients.

You will have to judge the objectivity of an ex-patient, and the relevance of his comments, for your situation. You should note, too, the clues you can directly or indirectly observe or infer in his behavior as well as what he says.

But with all the caution one must use in considering this source of information about therapists—and all others—it is our strong belief that some information, as comprehensive and as objective as you can make it, is better than none in selecting professional help for you and your child. Your information can usefully supplement whatever a referring source or agency may recommend. Ultimately, you must make the choice and judge its effectiveness for yourself.

Where to Get Professional Help

Public agencies and private practitioners are the main sources for obtaining professional help with children, although there are also some private agencies that fall somewhere in between these two for advantages and disadvantages. The public sector is growing much faster than the private; government-supported clinics and centers are blanketing an increasing number of our states, city schools and hospitals are rapidly expanding their thera-peutic services to children, and federally subsidized pro-grams are bringing services to ordinarily neglected areas and groups.

The public services are growing so explosively because private services obviously have been so limited in coverage and so costly to the individual. Making free or inexpensive public services widely available does not, of course, increase the supply of trained practitioners, nor does it make services less expensive. It provides more therapists only in the sense that it generally encourages persons other than psychologists and psychiatrists—including students—to practice treatment, and the whole community pays extra taxes for it, instead of the individual's paying the fee. In fact, the per-hour cost of treatment in a clinic or agency often runs higher than in private practice because there is more paper work, there are more staff meetings, lectures, and consultations, and there are other ancillary activities such as supervision, training, and agency contacts.

There are advantages and disadvantages to you in seeking help from a public clinic, center, or agency. The most obvious advantage is the cost. The services are free or quite inexpensive, often being based upon income. In Minnesota, for example, many public centers charge an hourly fee of 1 percent of your federal income tax, up to a specified maximum. Another advantage is that certain minimum standards of competence are required by the hiring agent, and the agency tends to be more sensitive to gross incompetence than is a state accrediting body for private practitioners.

A third advantage of the public agency or clinic presumably is the "team" approach. We say "presumably" because there is no evidence that group practice by different disciplines produces any better results. In fact, apparently the one well-controlled published research project on the subject (by D. N. Wiener and O. N. Raths, in April, 1959, American Journal of Orthopsychiatry) indicates no advantages at all for the team approach to psychological problems, and it is a far more costly and time-consuming process than is seeing just one professional man.

Other advantages of the agency are that it can provide better follow-up with other community resources, more time for the individual client, and better control of the individual practitioner's peculiarities. These, too, are somewhat dubious advantages. They are likely to exist in a very well run organization, but quite unlikely to exist in a mediocre or poorly run one. Ideally publicly supported centers would not be under the same pressure as the private practitioner to run patients through on an hourly assembly line. Ideally they need not produce income or big case-loads, but only provide an excellent service to the community. However, they are often judged solely by the number of clients they see, and as a result are eager to produce big case-loads without evaluating their results. It is a rare public agency (or private practitioner) that can produce figures on how many children's problems have been solved and what they were, and proof that they were solved.

As far as the practitioner's idiosyncracies are concerned, it seems likely that when he is working constantly with others he is less likely to go off in peculiar directions or to become arrogant and rigid than when he is in practice by himself, unobserved by colleagues and unable to interact with others about difficulties he encounters. These are real problems in the practice of human behavior change methods. It is all too easy for a therapist to begin to feel he is practically infallible, to blame his mistakes on his patients, and to begin to practice off-beat methods that he judges by his belief rather than by results. These dangers are small, but are more likely to be controlled in group practice than in private.

There are also disadvantages, however, to getting help from public organizations—whether clinic, school, university, hospital, or ghetto storefront. For one, you are less likely to get the best individual practitioners. Even those who work in public organizations are unlikely to have much time for new clients, and they probably spend most of their time consulting, training, and supervising. You are much more likely to get a student in training, who is getting experience by working with you. Even though he is often receiving some supervision between his sessions with you, he is, after all, just learning his profession, and agency clients are considered fair game for his experience.

You will also usually waste far more time being "processed" in a public organization than in individual private practice. Often you will have to go through preliminary interviews with one or more professionals before you are considered for treatment, a process that may take several hours. It may be several weeks before you can finally get the professional help. Often an agency or clinic takes more hours, and covers more weeks to be *evaluated* for help, than to get the help you actually need. Contrast this process with consulting an individual private practioner, who can see you directly and may try to offer you help immediately. *(Group* practice, even though private, may have the same disadvantages as a public organization.)

A final disadvantage of group practice, public or private, is that it cannot as easily insure the privacy and confidentiality of your contacts as can a private practitioner. Whether such privacy is desirable is another matter. Usually patients exaggerate the necessity for such privacy, and there are even disadvantages to it, touched on elsewhere. But if you want your privacy insured, it is much less likely to be preserved where your file is kept in a general office, where various clerical and professional help have access to it, where it may be used for research and training purposes, and where your case may be subject to general discussion within the organization.

Getting the Most Out of Professional Help

Regardless of where you go for professional help, you can get more from it if you ask for what you want as specifically as possible, if you listen carefully and modify your requests as you learn in therapy, if you try to make your counselor work for you as hard and as efficiently as possible, and if you continuously elicit, try out, evaluate results of, and modify your attitudes and behavior from suggestions for solutions that can be devised during your therapy.

What you need most are solutions to the problem you are encountering with your child, and you want to get these solutions as soon as possible. If you can avoid it, you do not want your therapy to extend any longer than necessary, to involve any more of your life or thought than necessary. If certain habits and attitudes of yours are contributing to the problem and you must determine what they are and change them, you want to do this as efficiently as possible. You do not want to extend your analysis of causes and determination of solutions over a period of years if months will do. You do not want to have to analyze your own past back to your childhood, if you can solve the problem by analyzing and changing your present behavior.

The preponderance of research evidence today indicates that direct, short-term, current-problem-directed help is at least as effective and long-lasting as long-term, indirect help involving analysis of the past—and it is a great deal more efficient, taking much less of your time and energy and often of your money. The more specific your questions and requests for direct help, and the more the help you receive is directed to provide immediate, specific solutions to current problems, the more likely it is that you will be able to settle and keep settled your current problems with your child. It also seems likely that such a direct-action approach will provide you with the attitudes and methods to solve efficiently the succession of new problems that constantly arise with your children.

Often it is up to you to set the pace for your therapy in this direction. Your counselor will seldom feel the pressure to devise immediate solutions as keenly as you do. Also, he may get somewhat lazy in his practices, and not really care as acutely as you do how long the treatment takes. He may get tired of his work, and loaf. He will seldom work as hard to help you find solutions as he is capable of working, and he and you can profit from his being intelligently and reasonably prodded a bit.

Nor should you worry about changing therapists when this appears reasonable to you. You do not want to change impulsively or in a fit of anger or annoyance. But if, over a period of weeks, you do not think you are getting help and if your therapist can provide no likelihood of help and cannot specify the measures you should take, you should feel free to make a change. The change should not necessarily mean much loss because of needing to aquaint a new practitioner with your problem. If there was profit in your previous therapy, it should be carried within you when you shift to the new man. You would then build with the new help upon what you had previously received. What you carry in you, not what your previous counselor learned about you, should be what counts most, *if* you always demand as concrete help as possible right from the beginning of your therapy.

This is not to say that you do not need to be patient. You cannot change habits of years' standing in a few weeks. Even if your therapist can suggest reasonable solutions a few sessions after he begins seeing you, it may take you weeks or months to try them out, to follow up on them, to adjust and change them as necessary, and to make the solutions permanent. You must work hard to succeed, and no therapist can make important behavior change easy or comfortable.

You need not function on the basis either of blind faith in your therapist or of impulsiveness in following your own feelings. You can ask for concrete suggestions to try out, you can tell whether you are trying them out and discuss what the results are, and you can change or not according to reasonable judgments about results or prospects of results.

Integrating Professional Help

You cannot indiscriminately accept and apply all the help you may be offered or ask for. From different sources—even from the same source at different times—it may be vague, contradictory, offensive to your values, insensitive, or simply too incomplete or superficial because of not taking into consideration as much as you know or want to include.

Still, in the face of a stubborn, persisting problem, you should try out as wide a range of solutions as seems reasonable. You alone, however, can encompass all necessary considerations in the decisions and procedures you apply. You will have to coordinate and select from the suggestions from school, church, professionals, and non-professionals. You will have to give direction and consistency to the course of action you decide on.

Suppose, for example, the problem you take to the psychologist is your son's distractibility in school, which, the teacher has reported to you, makes him unable to learn up to his ability. The private psychologist recommends that distractions at school be held to a minimum especially for your son, and that his lessons be simplified more than usual, as far as possible, by insisting that he complete the smallest segments before he can move on to anything else.

Even if you are not aware of a similar problem at home, the principle of training involved can be extended to his activities at home, with probable benefit for the problem at school. At home also, he can be held to completion of the simplest tasks before he is allowed to take on others, or to putting away each toy before he is allowed to play with another. He would thus be trained, *wherever possible*, in concentrating and completing each activity and not be permitted the slack that got him labeled distractible in the first place.

Who will work with the teacher to coordinate the psychologist's advice, and neighborhood parents who might observe your son's play activities from time to time? The psychologist may not want to spend his time at such a task—or you may not want to pay for his time to do so.

Often, then, it will fall to you, as the parent who sought the help with the problem, to plan, in conjunction with the professional person you consult, how to coordinate the various contexts in which your child is developing his habits, in order to make the change effort as efficient as possible. It will then be your task to implement and follow up on the plan to insure its success.

PART II

TRAINING IN SELF-DISCIPLINE

CHAPTER VI

The Judicious Use
of Psychological Tests

PSYCHOLOGICAL TESTS HAVE been used in education and psychology for many decades. Let us see how these instruments and techniques developed, what their strengths and weaknesses are, and how they can be of help to you or your child in solving problems.

How Tests Began

Psychological tests began in a very practical way. The public schools of Paris at the turn of the twentieth century were faced, as all schools are, with decisions about how to place youngsters according to their abilities. A physician-psychologist, Alfred Binet, began to work on this problem from the standpoint of finding items or test questions that could predict how a child would learn in a school setting. He experimented with all kinds of problems and questions —including many that he had to discard—and ended up with the first intelligence test.

This test, known as the Binet-Simon Test, and later, in its modified American version, as the Stanford-Binet Intelligence Test, was an early landmark in psychological testing.

The functions of a test are to get some measure of "ability" (usually of some specifically designated sort, such as "verbal ability" or "mechanical ability") that presumably is not influenced much by experience or special training. We say "presumably" because there can be no "pure" tests of ability, entirely uninfluenced by experience or training. What we seek in most tests, however, is some measure of ability that is not specifically related to any given experience. For example, we know that some children untutored in music can be shown to have "perfect pitch" or a very accurate pitch discrimination. They were not taught this discrimination; it appears to be unlearned, although it might have been influenced by some (unspecific) experiences. Also, it is difficult to teach pitch discrimination to one who has a very low acuity or sensitivity in this area of experience. Discrimination accuracy can be taught to some extent, and refinements can be made, but a large gain in pitch discrimination is not likely. Nor would one single out pitch discrimination to teach in order that a person become a professional musician; with poor pitch discrimination in the first place (untutored), one is unlikely to try to improve it in order to become an accomplished violinist or singer. On the other hand, one would want to learn how to speak and read a foreign language in order to become a specialist in the culture and politics of some foreign country, despite little initial ability or interest in learning languages.

To many psychologists, the meaning of "ability" is ambiguous because there are so many cases in human affairs where the so-called ability can be taught. We do not really know the limits of human ability, nor are we likely to discover them soon. Understanding of ability depends a great deal upon how it is studied and how it is used. For example, when the first crude typewriters were made, one's typing speed was severely limited even though one might have high ability in the area of finger dexterity. As better typewriters were made, one's "ability" increased and the ceiling for typing speed rose considerably. Who knows how much human ability can be extended by increasing the effectiveness and efficiency of instruments!

In the area of sprinting and long distance running, also, the ability picture keeps changing. Once it was thought that sprinters could not run the 100-yard dash in less than 9.6 seconds, and that the mile could not be run in less than four minutes. Both of these "records," supposedly at the upper limit of human ability, have been beaten numerous times in recent years. Has human ability increased? Was the ability there and just not used? How do we regard this elusive matter of ability?

Often teachers and psychologists remark that "Johnny has lots of ability, but he doesn't use it" or "Mary's musical ability is great, if she would just practice more" or "Most children have much more ability than they ever use in school" or "Human beings seldom use more than 20 to 30 percent of their mental ability."

Ability is not some hard-rock, irreducible, unaffected quantum of knowledge, skill, or circumstance. No one really knows what ability someone possesses except as that someone uses, develops, or perfects what he can do.

Among all the people in Africa, there are almost certainly many with "musical ability," "artistic ability," and other "abilities" comparable to what one would find in Europe or the United States, but in Africa these abilities often do not show themselves in ways that our culture can evaluate. We can only infer their wide range of ability in any field among any large groups of people in the world, and what is needed to develop the ability (or capacity) is schooling, training, cultural influences, and attitudes that bring human potentialities to their fruition—along with different ways of judging the achievements of different cultures.

In substance, we judge one's ability by what he actually does—not by what some presumably pure, uninvolved, unequivocal test says. Even in the case of music, where hereditary factors perhaps play a higher role than in other cases, we do not know how well one can discriminate sounds and pitches in playing or singing except by cultivating the person's skills and encouraging him to reach his limits.

So the quest for "basic abilities" and "natural capacity" is really likely to be meaningless. Too many parents have been beguiled into inaction regarding a child's achievement problems at school because they have been told the child has excellent basic ability—even though it is not used. They are at least partially satisfied and pleased to know that the ability is there. They then wait for it to show itself, to be released by some natural development or inspired teacher, rather than asking what can be done to help the child discipline himself and develop the habits necessary for achievement and productivity. (See Chapter IV.)

Achievement More Important Than Ability

In contrast to the notion of ability as some "pure" condition is the more practical and workable notion related to achievement as measured by various indices. In this view, what really counts is what the child can do, or what he can learn to do under proper educational guidance (see Chapter IV).

The concept of achievement can be applied to almost any human activity—reading, arithmetic, information about history, geography, or English; sports; or such unusual areas as knowledge about how the Egyptian bodies were "mummified" or how primitive man forged his tools. Achievement may be as remarkable and esoteric—or as commonplace—as human interests and efforts.

There are countless numbers of tests to measure achievement. Any school or child psychologist can and sometimes, unfortunately, does administer a battery of tests long enough to keep a child busy for weeks. A few years ago, when schools and teachers stressed testing more than today, batteries of tests many, many hours long were given to children. Even recently, some test batteries—mostly achievement tests—have taken up to 35 or 40 hours of children's time. This endless repetition (and duplication) of testing is nonproductive, except, perhaps, for research purposes. Today a good, economical, and useful battery of tests should take only a few hours once some practical purpose is clearly defined. We shall discuss this further when considering some details of test results.

Achievement tests cover what one has learned formally or informally. Suppose we give a child a reading test. It covers what he has learned from his reading instruction (or, perhaps, what he has picked up for himself, if we are talking about a preschool child or one who has had minimal schooling). Perhaps he reads at the "3.6 grade level," meaning he reads about halfway between the third and fourth grades compared to average children, perhaps throughout the nation, on this test. Spelling achievement, or any other area of knowledge, can be measured in the same way.

Achievement test results are useful to compare with how a child is actually doing in school. The tests provide a formal measurement of a child's achievement compared with how he is performing on a daily basis. Some children learn more than their daily school performance indicates because they read widely, listen carefully, or pick up much information in ways other than through formal (classroom) presentation. A child may be failing at school in reading, for example, but upon being tested might demonstrate substantial reading skill. We would assume that he had the skill—he has shown this on the test—but that the conditions in the classroom (perhaps absence of sufficiently positive reinforcing conditions) did not bring this skill into play with the daily work. This results in a problem for the teacher, but it is one for the parent, also, once he knows his child needs more stimulation and encouragement for the school work.

Achievement test results may be useful, too, in picking up a child's relatively strong and weak points. One child achieves well in arithmetic but poorly in spelling and reading; another child achieves in the opposite pattern. If a youth is headed for what he hopes will be a career in engineering or physical science, then his achievement in arithmetic and quantitative reasoning will be especially important. A youngster expecting to study the law or to enter almost any profession requiring extended schooling would need to show good achievement in verbal areas such as vocabulary, reading, and word usage. Achievement patterns become of ever greater importance with the older youngster about to enter formal advanced training for his life's vocational work.

Special Aptitude Tests

There are special aptitude areas, too, that are of importance—"aptitude" suggesting a relatively natural, basic, and undeveloped potential. These include such achievement or skill areas as spatial relations and abstract reasoning. Spatial relations would be important to the potential engineer or physical scientist, also perhaps to the aviator and the navigator on a ship. This is an area that deals with the relationships of geometric space, especially in relation to stationary or moving objects. Abstract reasoning, in contrast to concrete reasoning, pivots on seeing relationships between objects or conditions and being able to draw inferences or conclusions from them.

Sometimes the term "aptitude" is used interchangeably with "ability." The same comments apply to both: one should not think of it in relation to some rock-bottom level, but in terms of how it can be used effectively in achieving specified goals. Frequently children do not show much aptitude for abstract and spatial concepts, because they have not been exposed to such areas of skill, but when opportunity develops, skills also do.

An example of the kind of item appearing on a spatial relations test would be as shown in Figure 1.

Figure 1: Examples of *spatial relations* **test items.**

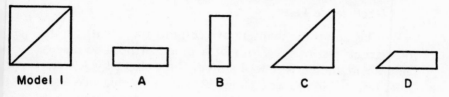

Which design (A, B, C, or D) can be formed directly from model 1?
(Answer: C)

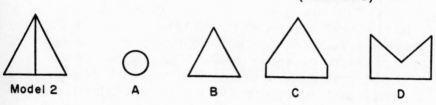

Which design (A, B, C, or D) is closest in *pattern* to model 2 ?
(Answer: B)

An example of the kinds of items appearing on an abstract reasoning test is shown in Figure 2.

Figure 2: Examples of *abstract reasoning* **test items.**

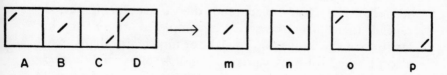

Which figure (m, n, o, or p) completes the design stated in A-D?
(Answer: m)

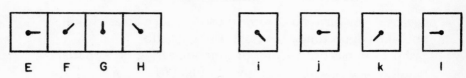

E   F   G   H   i   j   k   l

Which figure (i, j, k, l) completes the design stated in E-H?

(Answer: l)

Intelligence Tests

We began this chapter by commenting that early intelligence testing grew out of a practical need to place children in the Paris school system. This effort by Alfred Binet resulted in the well-known American intelligence test named the Stanford-Binet. The way such a test is made up is the concern of this section, to convey to you what intelligence testing really means.

Individual intelligence tests (more reliable than group tests) generally consist of five to ten or so subtests. For example: *Vocabulary* (defining words, beginning with very simple words for young children—"hat," "dress," "car," "spoon," and the like); *General Information* (for example: "Who is the President of the United States?" "What does a car use as fuel?" "How far is it from New York to San Francisco?"; *Verbal Reasoning* ("What does this saying mean: 'Two wrongs do not make a right'?" "Why do busy traffic intersections have traffic lights or policemen?" "Why does water run downhill?"); *Arithmetic* ("How much is six dollars and ten dollars?" "How many apples could you buy for 48¢ if each apple cost 12¢?"); *Digit Memory* or *Repetition* (the examiner says digits, one per second, in a clear voice, and the subject being tested repeats them after the series is completed—these vary in length from two digits up to eight or nine digits; digits may also be asked for backwards); *Symbol Memory* or *Learning* (here the subject is given a "code" relating numbers and symbols, such as 1 2 3 4 and after practicing the code
X H 3 ៣

for a few number-symbol combinations, he is expected to do as many as he can in a limited period of time, such as one or two minutes); *Identifying Missing Parts of Pictures* (this test presents a series of common objects—such as a flag, a chair, a house—with an important part missing, and the subject is to identify the missing part); *Assembling Mixed-up Series of Pictures* (sometimes called *Picture Arrangement*, this test presents a series of pictures that tells a story when properly arranged in sequence; the original pictures are scrambled and the subject is to arrange them properly); *Memory for Designs or Figures* (the subject is presented for a brief period of time—say five to ten seconds—geometric forms of a generally unfamiliar type, which he is to reproduce from memory when the model has been taken away).

Other types of subtests may be used, depending upon the theory of intelligence or upon some practical ends which guide the test-maker. Not all tests have the same composition. For example, the Stanford-Binet is mainly verbal in makeup and, while useful for many purposes, is more limited because of its language requirements than the Wechsler tests, which are constructed more along the lines described above. In any case, the Stanford-Binet and the Wechsler Intelligence Scales for Children (WISC) are by far the most widely used of the individual intelligence measures for children and provide highly correlated measures of I.Q. (intelligence quotient).

What Is an I.Q.?

No discussion of tests and testing would be complete without some reference to the ubiquitous I.Q. There has been much controversy in both professional and lay circles about the I.Q.—what it means and what its proper uses are.

The term "I.Q." means "Intelligence Quotient." The quotient is a score much like the scores discussed in the early pages of this chapter. Specifically, the I.Q. is obtained by comparing the child's "mental age" to his life age or chronological age. A test is given which allows the child to earn points or credits. These credits are stated in terms of how the average child of a given age performs— the so-called mental age. If the child's mental age is higher than his life age, he scores above average. Say a six-year-old scores as well as the average eight-year old. His mental age would be eight years. Dividing his mental age (eight) by his life age (six) would give the I.Q.: 8/6 is 1.33; multiplying by 100 (that is, taking away the decimal point) gives the child with this score an I.Q. of 133. If the child earned scores or points equal to the average nine-year-old and he was only seven in life age, the fraction would be 9/7 or a 129 I.Q. Correspondingly, if the child scores *below* his life age, he will get an I.Q. below 100, which is average. For example, if a nine-year-old scores only at a level equal to that of the average six-year-old, he is doing only about two-thirds as well as the average; hence his I.Q. is 67.

The I.Q., like other test scores, is most accurately reported in terms of a band or range. One usually thinks of a child's score as included in a range of about ten I.Q. points. If a child obtained an I.Q. of 95, we would say, on the basis of knowing how tests are constructed, used, and interpreted, that the chances are he would score most of the time between 90 and 100 I.Q., which is within the normal range.

Tests bearing the I.Q. label are not used as indiscriminately as they once were. In addition, when they are properly used, the reporting of the score is usually not solely in terms of an I.Q. score, but as a descriptive range such as the following:

Bright Normal   I.Q. range 100 to 110 (or 115)

Superior   I.Q. range 110 (or 115) to 125 (or 130)

One could go on to add other descriptive labels for still higher scores. For lower scores, the following designations are often used:

Low Normal	I.Q. 85 or 90 to 100
Slow Learning	I.Q. 75 or 80 to 90
Borderline	I.Q. 65 or 70 to 75
Retarded	I.Q. 65 (some use 70) or below

These are used for descriptive and administrative purposes, such as deciding whether to consider placing a child in a "slow learning," "retarded," or "special education" class.

How Good Are Tests?

People often ask how good tests are. This is, of course, an important question, but the answer is somewhat indirect. Tests have no *inherent* value—they are good only to the extent that they serve some useful purpose. Such purposes might include predicting later achievement, providing a basis for dividing a population into those most likely to learn quickly vs. those who are slower-learning (a common use in school settings), and accurately describing the present status of one's intellectual functioning (of value, for example, in seeing how well an accident victim is functioning for purposes of vocational and educational guidance, or how well a foreign person might do in an English-language setting).

How good tests are depends also upon whether they yield reliable or reproducible results. If a test gave a widely different score each time it was used on the same person, it would be confusing and perhaps useless. How would one know which result to believe? If you measured your sofa several times for a slip cover and got considerably different results each time you took the measurement, you would not know what you had, nor how to proceed. It is the same with an educational or psychological measurement (test).

Another criterion of how good a test is hinges on how well it does what it is supposed to do—that is, how well it lives up to its name. If a test is called a measure of intelligence or mechanical aptitude, it should relate to that kind of performance in a school, training, or work situation. If a test called "mechanical aptitude" does not differentiate between students in an engineering curriculum and those in an art school or a music school, it is probably not a very good test. It is not doing what it purports to do—test for mechanical aptitude.

Tests have been known to have the wrong name, so to speak. A test may be devised to do a given job, but turn out to do a different job much better. One clerical test, for example, seems to measure general intelligence better than it predicts clerical skill. The fact that a test bears a given name is no assurance that it will do as the name implies.

Tests are measurements as well as "tests." We commonly say that we "test" someone to see what he knows about history or English. But we also do more than that: we measure how much he knows in terms of some criterion—grade level, percentile mark, I.Q., or the like.

Measurements

There are several kinds of measurements a test may yield. Suppose your child is given a reading test. What are the results? The test should tell you several things, depending upon what the test is capable of doing and upon the skill of the examiner. One yield is that of a "score"—he got 26 right out of 50, after reading a paragraph. "But what does this score mean?" you might ask. Does it mean he did well, poorly, or average? It so happens that he scored in the average range, but one would not know that from the score alone. This is why we say a test has to yield more than a score—to have meaning, the score must be put in some kind of context, or place the particular child in relation to others in his age or class group.

There are several ways in which a score might be placed in a broader context. One is for a grade level score to be provided. The child in question got 26/50 items; this put him at grade level 3.7, or 7/10 of the way between grade 3 and grade 4, a little better than the half-year mark (3.5 grade level) in reading for the average child in the third grade.

Another way in which a score can be made meaningful is to give it a percentile rank. In this case, the people who take the test are ranked from the highest (99th percentile, or 100th percentile) to the lowest (1 percentile or 0 percentile). All the ranks in between are filled in depending upon the score. One who ranked at the 25th percentile (25%-ile) did better than 25 percent, but not as well as the 75 percent above the score. Likewise, one scoring at the 85th percentile (85%-ile) has done better than 85 percent but not as well as the top 15 percent. And so on for any score. Many of the achievement tests taken in schools today put the child's score in some percentile term, as Figure 3 shows.

Figure 3. Graph showing percentile ranks.

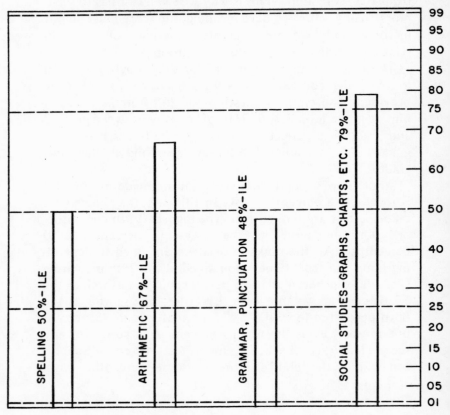

A child's score is shown in terms of a percentile figure. For example, this child showed the following: Spelling 50th percentile; Arithmetic 67th percentile; Grammar, Punctuation 48th percentile; and Social Studies—Reading Charts, Graphs, etc.—79th percentile. This child's scores were obtained when he was in the fifth grade; grade-level scores could also have been considered (Spelling, 4.5 grade level; Arithmetic, 4.8 grade level; Grammar 4.4 grade level; Social Studies, 5.1 grade level).

Sometimes the percentile score is stated in terms of larger intervals than the single percentile score, that is, put in terms of the "upper tenth" or "lower tenth" or "upper quartile" or "middle quartile." This way of reporting a score centers on the *range* within which the score falls rather than on the specific score. It is probably a more valid way of reporting a test score. Stating a child's performance in terms of a range correctly suggests that he does not make the same score (say, the 51st percentile) each time, but tends to score within a range of, say, 10-15 percentile points above and below that figure. Saying that a child scored in the third quartile (the third 25-percentile range—that is, between the 50th and 75th percentiles) gives us a range or approximation that is more accurate than saying that he scored at exactly the 62nd percentile. Figure 4 shows how the percentile range (or quartile) is reported on a test a child has taken.

Fig. 4. Graph of quartile and decile scores.

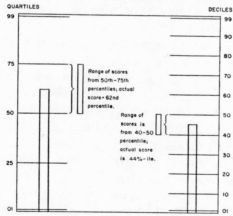

Quartile scores or ranges are on the lefthand side and decile scores on the righthand side. This child scored at the 62nd percentile on an English test, shown on the left (range is from 50th to 75th percentile) and at the 44th percentile on Arithmetic (on the right of the graph, showing range of scores between 40th and 50th percentiles).

Sometimes the whole range of test results is divided into deciles (or 10-percentile units or ranges). Here the "upper decile" or 91st to 99th percentile is the highest score range, whereas the "lowest decile" or lowest 10 percent range is between the first percentile and the 10th percentile. A child scoring on a given test in the "fourth decile" would fall between the 41st and 49th percentile. Here, again, the decile form of reporting suggests that test scores are best described within a range rather than with a specific point. The righthand side of the graph shows the decile ranges, the lefthand side the quartile ranges.

Other measurements also are used, but these are the most common.

Can Tests Predict Accurately?

This question is related to the one asked earlier as to whether tests are valid. Tests can usually predict better than chance what they have been constructed to predict, although not with complete accuracy.

If one were on a committee to pick the students most likely to succeed academically, he would want to know each child's record up to that time and also how well the child did on valid tests. (If the test is not valid, there is no use in giving it at all, so we are assuming that our tests do well what they purport to do, although in fact many do not.) Generally speaking, the best prediction of what one will do in the future is what he has done in the past, *assuming that no unusual changes occur in the child or the environment.* Students who do well in high school generally do better in college than those whose high school record is poor.

Achievement tests attempt to assess in a fair way what a person knows (or what his skill level is) at a given time, which is a distillation of what he has done heretofore in his classes. A comprehensive test on American history would be a distillation and a sampling of all the history courses in, say, high school; the same for French, mathematics, or any other course. These tests attempt to cover, in a way more fair than any the classroom teacher can usually employ, what the youth knows about a given subject-matter area. The result provides the best prediction of what he will do in subsequent courses (assuming that motivation and interest are present, an assumption one has to make in judging any human situation). The test is just a shorthand way of assessing the student's potential.

Recently we attended a horse show for youngsters who had been trained in riding. The show was based in part on contests involving jumping, cantering, trotting, and other skills horsemen can display. The purpose of the show and the contests was to pick from among several dozen contestants the best six to represent the geographic area in a state-wide horse show to be held a few weeks later. One could have tossed coins to pick the best horsemen, or asked the riders a few questions, or judged the beauty of the horses, or used other means to assess ability, most of which would not have been valid for the given purpose.

The "tests" the horsemen were given were those most closely related to what experienced horsemen have always considered to be "good horsemanship." These contests were tests, just as much as the test the child takes to find out what he knows about American history or Spanish or mathematics. The horsemanship tests are subject to the same limitations as the school tests. The horsemanship tests are perhaps easier to assess and to work with, but in principle they are based on the same considerations of performance one has to use in evaluating mechanical skills, knowledge in various subject matter areas, and the like.

How accurately will the results of the horse show predict how well the chosen horsemen will compete in the state-wide show? No one knows with complete accuracy. All we can say is that, given reasonable fairness and equality in opportunity to compete, those chosen as the best performers in our local show will probably be the best performers in the large show, or at least will compete on a level comparable to the way they have in the past. Horsemen come up with "scores" (points or credits earned for various activities), and these are predictive of future performance. We are carrying out tests and measurements with the horsemen just as we are with the schoolchild in his academic work.

The Profile

The test profile is simply a summary statement of all the tests taken, reported on a given chart and indicating a pattern of relative strengths and weaknesses. That is, if the student has taken the "Differential Aptitude Test" battery, all of these tests are reported on a single chart (profile). If a student has taken a battery (several subtests) such as the Stanford Achievement Test or the Metropolitan Achievement Test, these subtests are reported in some single form. Examples of these follow.

The tests (or subtests, meaning tests on parts of a larger battery or collection of tests) are here reported in percentile or decile form. The youngster being reported on showed the following profile scores:

Differential Aptitude Tests*

Mechanical Aptitude	30th percentile
Spatial Relations	22nd percentile
Numerical Reasoning	49th percentile
Verbal Reasoning	70th percentile
Abstract Reasoning	60th percentile
Language Usage	73rd percentile
Clerical Speed & Accuracy	40th percentile

---

*Differential Aptitude Test, Third Ed., by G. K. Bennett, H. G. Seashore, and A. G. Wesman, N. Y.: Psychological Corp., 1959.

All of these scores would then be "profiled" according to the actual percentile score earned.

A word should be said about the variation in scores. A child does not score equally well on all tests. He is, like all human beings, better in some activities than in others. This youngster was good in verbal skills (Verbal Reasoning and Language Usage) but average to poor in other Differential Aptitude Test scores. Another child might score just the opposite, still another one do well in all tests (but not have the same score in each case), and still another one do poorly in all tests. Also, the child does not get the same score on the same or similar tests year after year, or time after time; all scores tend to vary in a given range, but the likelihood of extreme changes in scores is very small. Given normal testing circumstances, good motivation in the child, and proper use of tests, the scores should be fairly similar from one time to another.

Tests and Diagnosis

Tests are used to indicate at what level a child is performing at a given time. In addition, tests are used to "diagnose" the individual. What does "diagnose" mean in this sense?

A reading test may be "diagnostic" in that it points up the strong and weak areas of the child's reading skills and performances. It may tell us that his "word attack" skills are weak, or that he confuses vowels in reading and in pronunciation, or that he has trouble with suffixes. Arithmetic tests may "diagnose" in the sense that they show that the child has good arithmetic reasoning but makes careless errors in computation, that he does not know the multiplication tables, or that he has not learned how to use exponents in first-year algebra. The diagnoses in these cases are not used to show illness or pathology, but simply relative strengths and weaknesses. This is generally a useful result if the tests are in good hands and if proper use is made of them in the classroom, leading to constructive action.

Sometimes a *battery* of tests is also used diagnostically. That is, tests in the verbal areas are compared with tests dealing with quantitative relations. The latter would be found in arithmetic computation and reasoning, the former in vocabulary, analogies, and reasoning. A wide battery of tests would probably include tests of both a verbal and a quantitative nature, as these appear to be major subdivisions of school learning. In addition, as the child gets older and develops skills in other areas (abstract reasoning, mechanical reasoning, spatial relations), these areas also are included in batteries of tests.

The "profile," discussed earlier in this chapter, is really a way of presenting a "diagnostic picture" of the child's areas of knowledge and skill. The profile charts his scores in various fields, such as the academic areas studies in school or the aptitude areas which are not necessarily closely related to school courses. By placing the child's scores on a profile chart, we know whether he scored in the upper or lower ranges compared to others of his age or with his degree of training.

Sometimes personality factors influence test scores, and this fact is used diagnostically. For example, a child who is readily distracted and has trouble concentrating on new learning materials may do poorly on tests requiring immediate memory or recall; he may do poorly on tests that require him to concentrate well and repeat digits, words, or sentences. For instance, some individual tests of intelligence require the child to repeat a series of digits, read to him one at a time and one per second. If he is very distractible, he may have trouble keeping these digits in mind and repeating them accurately. Similarly for repeating sentences, such as the following: "The cows were grazing in the green fields when the farmer went out to look for them." One can get a general idea of the sentence, but he may leave out the descriptive words such as "green" fields, or may replace the word "farmer" with "the man."

Tests of immediate memory and tests relating to visual designs (geometric figures) are often related to brain damage (or to conditions often thought to be basically due to brain damage or to some other neurological problem, not well specified or understood). It is often surprising to see how distorted a geometric design can become when a child with learning problems (perhaps due to birth injuries, to a high temperature associated with an illness, or to some accident) is asked to take a test of this type. The details are changed, the overall design is not preserved, and the connecting parts are noticeably altered. The following is a ten-year-old child's distorted drawing from memory of a design:

When a child is given a series of such designs and when his performance, compared to that of the normal child, is consistently in the direction of unusual distortions or errors, we must conclude that he does not "see" the designs as a normal person does and hence there are likely also to be some more general effects on his learning. In the school situation, of course, his learning problems will usually show up clearly.

Besides for various kinds of distortion and for purposes of educational selection, however, a wide battery of tests may prove useful in guiding the child in his studies. We have found at the college level, and to a lesser extent at the senior high school level, that many youngsters who think they are interested in engineering do not in fact test in a way that would support this expressed interest. They may like to "tinker" with tools and equipment, make things, put models together, but they appear to lack the conceptual skills and the abstract and mathematical reasoning which underlie engineering performance. They misread a small amount of skill and over-generalize to the big picture which is engineering. A similar description applies to youngsters who fancy they would like to be musicians—they may have some elementary qualifications but lack the more subtle skills needed for good or expert musicianship. One could generalize to all professional areas in this way. Such youth need to have a a good solid review of skills and potentialities and go from there to educational planning. For the frustrated engineer there is always a vast area of related work such as applied mechanics, instrument repair, field work as a surveyor. Less demanding professional careers exist in music as well, and in all professional areas.

Describing a Wide Battery of Tests

References have been made thus far to various individual tests, and to concepts of ability, aptitude, and achievement. What would be most useful would be tests covering the widest possible variety of human educational and training (educational) concerns or objectives; problems concerning ability and whether it is learned or native are of secondary importance. We are concerned here with describing wide-ranging tests (a battery) that would be of specific as well as general significance and practical usefulness for most students.

For the young child, a general intelligence test such as the Stanford-Binet or the Wechsler Intelligence Scale for Children would be essential. From either of these tests, we would learn something of the child's general learning capability, how he compared in performance potential with his peers, and the subtests on which he did relatively well or poorly.

Some type of reading tests would be appropriate for the child in the first three grades. These would include reading for word identification, for paragraph meaning (answering questions on the basis of paragraphs read), and for drawing inferences from what one has read (drawing conclusions, as contrasted with answering factual questions).

As the child moves up the elementary ladder, other tests relating to specific subject matter fields would be included: spelling, arithmetic, comprehension (or reasoning), arithmetic computation, social studies (or history), language (includes grammar, punctuation, verb-subject agreement). Additional achievement tests in specific math courses (algebra, geometry), in foreign languages, and in certain history areas might be included at the high school level.

At the high school level, one should also assess interests by the Kuder Vocational Interest Test or the Strong Vocational Interest Blank. Some interests are still very subtle during the high school years, and it may be helpful to draw out by systematic questioning, as these interest tests do, the widest possible range of activities and preferences.

Study habits inventories are also important. The student's poor study techniques (or good techniques, if they are apparent) should be observed critically as closely as possible so that they can be improved.

Many students enroll in high school and college courses

out of inaccurate readings of their preferences. Being guided by an interest inventory is no guarantee that correct choices of subject matter will result, but adding relevant information to any situation is likely to be helpful. Also, the interest inventories point up relationships among interest areas that may not have been noticed before the testing (for example, between literary and science interests, or human welfare interests in conjunction with office and stenographic.)

Special attention might be given to a battery for the student who expresses interested in foreign languages, engineering, music, art, or any other specialized educational areas. Music and art are difficult to test for, but actual products in these areas might be evaluated, with ratings or judgments by music critics, teachers, and art connoisseurs. The latter are not tests in a rigorous psychological sense, but need to be relied upon in lieu of standarized testing, for the potentially creative student of art or music who wants to enter advanced training.

Predictive Value of Tests

Tests cannot predict very well how the student will achieve in advanced or specialized training, even though they are usually better than chance. Tests of intellectual functioning are correlated with school achievement about 15 to 25 percent better than chance would allow. Other tests probably do no better; some of them do less well. If, however, the testing is accompanied by judicious choice of curriculum or school, and if the test interpretations include counseling in study procedures, the choice of supportive or alternative courses or curricula, and periodic follow-up counseling, the predictive value of the tests can be enhanced considerably. This "open" system of using tests and test results in combination with any factors that can maximize achievement can produce a melding of tests, student aspirations, and institution or program goals.

CHAPTER VII

Techniques of Effective Training

WHILE THIS ENTIRE book is about effective training—or making educational efforts effective and efficient—this chapter will explicitly detail techniques and how to apply them to implement the efforts best.

Many times parents and teachers—indeed the whole of society, through educational institutions—expend effort to train and educate children but end with the feeling that the effort was not productive or, even if it were modestly successful, that it was not efficient. Why are effectiveness and efficiency so commonly limited in the training and education of children? What remedies can be proposed? When are we choosing sensible training or educational goals and when are we focusing on unreasonable ones?

Setting Goals the First Step

"Setting goals" is again our starting place. How can we judge what we do, or how useful or effective it is, if we do not have a purpose and an expectation to guide us? A goal, a standard, an outcome—such must be formulated.

One must start by formulating goals of some sort, no matter how crudely and tentatively. They will almost surely need correction, modification, or even scrapping as one goes along (as the child matures and develops), and it is good to review them continuously for possible change. Starting the child's education or training without goals in mind almost always produces wasteful, disappointing, or perhaps even injurious results. The lack of explicit, well-considered goals does not mean that the parent or teacher has successfully bypassed the problem of goals, but merely that he has not initially recognized their importance—and he will have to take goals into account sooner or later. It is like driving off with your gas tank nearly empty—you may ignore it for a while, but soon there will be an inconvenient reckoning, which could have been avoided by the exercise of foresight.

Help in Setting Goals

How can goals be set intelligently? Certainly the child's *age* should be considered. You don't set a goal of college education for a two-year-old as a serious, informed effort. You might reasonably plan in a general financial way for this eventuality (the money could be also used for any other kind of education or training), but this is too remote a goal and too vague in terms of the child's actual capabilities as one can know them at age two.

In this illustration a second criterion has been implied— *length of time* before the goal can be realized. For most of us the vast majority of goals are immediate ones. A few days, several weeks, perhaps some months may be covered to achieve the goal, but longer periods are exceptions. One often hears teachers and parents saying to youngsters, "What are your long-range goals?" or "You have to amount to something when you're *grown*—so you'd better not waste your time now!" Not only are many efforts to set long-range goals too vague for the child to imagine— they don't "grab" him in any meaningful way—but they cannot be visualized by the adults themselves in any specific ways. The adults cannot tell or show or exemplify (model) this kind of goal-setting for the child. For the most part, they are only using empty words. Parents often try to make the goal more meaningful by stretching it out into the future with a kind of slogan which says "long-range is most important" or something equally meaningless to the child.

Setting short-term goals is a better training and educational procedure. We want to set goals for now and the immediate future, based on present behavior. Improving grades *this* week, care of the dog *today*, the thank-you note to Uncle Jack *tonight*, returning the book to the library *tomorrow*, fixing the broken bike *this week-end*, and so on. Too mundane? Not really. If the child does not program himself to do these concrete matters *daily*, how can he grasp the importance of such vague processes as "preparing for the future" or "thinking where you're going to be 10 or 20 years from now"? Few adults reading this book can truthfully say that they are where they are today because they set themselves clear goals years ago!

We pay the rent at the beginning of the month, the credit card charges come due at the end of the month, the lease renewal is due at the end of the year. Most matters that move us are relatively close at hand.

Let the child know you expect him to complete tasks by a set time, usually within a few days. This *is* training. This *is* education.

If he is left to himself to dawdle and postpone, he will learn to delay as a general rule. You will be inadvertently reinforcing his dilatory and careless procedures if you do not make the goals specific, timely, and well-structured.

Another criterion for setting goals: set them at a level the child can, at least in principle, succeed at. You and I cannot jump over a hurdle seven feet high, no matter how hard we try or how well we train. It is too much to ask. The child is often set goals (by well-meaning but uninstructed adults) that are too high, that are unattainable: all A's in school, perfect manners in company, *never* using bad language, *never* needing reminding to do his studying or his chores, and so on. When these too-high goals are failed by the child, the parent tends to reaffirm the goals with "Haven't I told you before, time and time again, about grades?" (or whatever the subject is) and tends to grind the child down into further defeats, instead of changing the goal, making the approach to the goal more gradual, or otherwise improving the goal.

Implicit in the above discussion about goal-setting is that pursuit of the goal(s) should be *gradual*. Most of what we learn that is very complex (such as skills in language, music, reading) is acquired on a gradual basis. One does not learn to type overnight; one may recognize the keyboard and know where the characters are, but this is not the same as typing, which is defined as, say, 40 words per minute with no more than two mistakes, for a five-minute period.

Among psychologists and educators, the procedure of gradually acquiring some skill or knowledge is known as *shaping*, or as "successive approximations toward some goal." "Rome wasn't built in a day" is a more common rendition of the same idea.

If the child can make a little progress in his reading week by week, or in his piano playing from one lesson to another, these are good signs. Moreover—and this is also very important—they become evidence to the child himself that he is moving forward. This knowledge is *reinforcing* to the child *and* to the parent. The parent can see or hear the change for the better in the child's performance.

A word of caution: saying that progress is gradual, that weekly one might notice changes in the child's reading or piano playing, is not to be interpreted rigidly. It may take two weeks, or a month, for progress to become visible. The amount of time is considerably less important than the fact that there *is* some progress. The rate (speed) of progress is mostly an individual matter. The *steadiness* of progress is the really important criterion, whether the skill is simple or complex, whether the child is experienced or inexperienced, whether the child is bright, average, or dull.

One almost universal error in teaching children is the tendency to expect too much too soon, to try to get perfection quickly. Adults who are too rigid, too demanding of themselves and others, "perfectionistic," fail to see that change is usually accomplished gradually. Once grasped, this concept of gradualness makes teaching more effective.

Another important technique of goal-setting with children is that of *reinforcing* the child's efforts and gains. Notice that we specified both *efforts* and *gains*. One has to make the effort, of course, first; gradually the procedures produce, over time, the gains.

Suppose a child is learning to swim. First he has to get into the water. That is an effort requiring willingness, a readiness to take on the problem of developing the skill. Then, when he actually begins to paddle and hold himself above water for a while, he is in the shaping or gradual-approximating process. Here he needs punctual and firm reinforcement. Calling his attention to the fact that getting into the water doesn't hurt—in fact, it is fun!—can be reinforcing. Paddling, close as it is to other motor activities the child enjoys (running, jumping, breathing heavily upon exertion), also can be reinforcing. It is reinforcing, we know, because once done it increases the chances that the child will enter the water more readily, paddle less reluctantly, and make further gains the next time he is in the pool. And so on through the whole process of skillful swimming, from the beginning and halting point at the age of about four, out to the point at, perhaps, age 16 when he may be on the swimming team. What a long way he has gone, how much patience, gradual improvement, and reinforcement went into this performance over a twelve-year period. That is learning, training, education!

Reinforcement should be prompt. Delays in reinforcing

produce lapses in progress, because they fail to connect the behavior with its consequences. If, as many psychologists maintain, behavior is determined by its consequences, then the reinforcement (consequence) is crucially important, and properly applied increases the chances that the behavior we want to produce will improve subsequently.

Reinforcement should be related to the child's preferences or desires (or needs). Candy might be a good reinforcer, or the words "well done" said by a beloved person. Money, free time, a trip to the movies, having a friend stay overnight—these are all possible reinforcements, but the exact reinforcement used must be tailored to the child himself. You can use candy too much—the child may become sated. You can use money too often—and produce an indifferent attitude toward money. The privilege of staying overnight at a friend's house in a week or two may be too remote if the child is young.

The emphasis on reinforcement implies that we select the positive, the gainful to reinforce, and play down or ignore the unwelcome behavior. If we pay too much attention to the child's mistakes, if we only attend to him when he errs or gets into trouble, we set up a consequence (attention) that may well increase the very behavior we wish to get rid of. For example, if a child leans over too far forward when he dives into the swimming pool and we concentrate on this error, we are not providing him with the opportunity to perceive the correct behavior. We have to shape him gradually to lean less, and reinforce each small effort and gain toward standing correctly. We ignore the error in behavior not by pretending it does not exist, but by emphasizing the solutions (alternatives) to the incorrect behavior and "shape up" gradually the correct, welcome, to-be-reinforced behavior.

The fact that parents and teachers often fail to reinforce positive behavior is illustrated by the common complaint of adults that "I've told him a thousand times not to do that—and he still does it." "I can't seem to get it into his head that he's doing the wrong thing. He's stubborn or stupid." Here the parent is concentrating attention on the unwanted behavior, providing no alternatives for the child and not reinforcing any slight effort to improve.

Remarks as quoted above come from parents who realize that what they are doing is not productive. Why not change, then? Reinforcement for *the parent* will come from having the child do well, having the child change from unwanted behavior to gainful activity. What is more reinforcing for a parent than seeing the child do well? The parent can gain this reinforcement by making more realistic demands, by gradualism, by being a good reinforcer herself—and by getting the encouraging feedback from the child's improved performance.

The use of reinforcement implies a *contingency* (or a *condition*). One is reinforced if and when he does some required activity. The child is reinforced with candy *when* he finishes his arithmetic; he is reinforced with a trip to the movie *if* he has kept his room in order; and so forth. All reinforcement implies (and should make explicit) an "if you do this, then that will follow" relationship. To attempt to reinforce without a condition or contingency will waste effort. Sometimes a parent promises a child something if he will behave, or threatens him with something if he does not, when the promise or the threat means nothing to the child. The "something" has to have meaning to the child (that is, be reinforcing in its presence, or missed when absent), and this value lies with the child, not the parent.

Reinforcement must be distinguished from bribery or blackmail, too. Bribery is where the child—not the parent—holds the reinforcement contingency, where the child demands a particular reward for behaving a certain way, or he will behave in a way punishing to the parent. "If you don't give me candy—or money, or a new bike—I'll break your new vase—or hit the baby."

The parent must hold the reins, and provide meaningful

rewards. For example, the parent says, "I'll give you some extra money if you will mow the lawn this morning." The child might say, "I don't want the money and I don't want to mow the lawn." That leaves the parent in a quandary. What the parent assumed was a reward—money—does not serve the purpose. If, on the other hand, the child was saving money for a new bike, the contribution of the money to his "kitty" might well be reinforcing, but it would be offered as a contingency: "You can earn some extra money for your bike when you have finished mowing the lawn" (and, of course, specify the agreement in monetary terms).

Consistency is another important feature of goal-setting—and goal-achieving. You cannot reinforce only when you feel moved to do it. At least in the beginning, at the start of developing a new, complex skill, reinforcing the child's efforts should be very consistent and be provided every time he does what is wanted. Later, however, the reinforcing efforts can be thinned out, so that you are reinforcing only intermittently—but not losing consistency.

Consistency is important in setting a structure within which reinforcement can occur. For example, if you are setting a schedule (or structure) within which the child is to do his daily chores, his music practice, his homework, you set an overall schedule to include what he does before school, after school, and in the evening, and reinforce his activity at each of these times in specific ways. For example, if the child is reasonably punctual and reliable about handling his early morning chores before school (hanging up his pajamas, brushing teeth, putting dirty clothes in the hamper, for example) he is then free to buy a dessert at lunch or to watch a half-hour of TV upon arrival from school in the afternoon. If he then does his chores in the afternoon around the house (such as feeding the dog or bringing in the paper), he gets a second TV program, or chocolate milk at afternoon snack time, and so on throughout the day.

Such overall structure makes expectations firm and clear to the child, and provides satisfaction in his life. If the child is successful in his early morning routine, and gets reinforced for it, but lags in the evening, he has a place to build from and a place to improve. The effective part of the routine may also tell the parent what is needed in the evening to make that part of the routine day's schedule work better (for example, TV may not be the reinforcer in the evening, or a particular TV program might be better than the alternative ones, or a reading period with Father may be what is needed to help this end-of-the-day slump).

Some Additional Considerations

The training and educational procedures cited above (setting goals, matching goals carefully with age, sensitivity to the length of time needed to achieve goals, recognizing proper levels of tasks for the child, the gradual (or shaping) nature of progress toward goals, reinforcing judiciously, and consistency in overall stance) are basic to succeeding with the purposes described in this chapter. However, they are not the whole story. Other considerations must be mentioned:

1. Gain the child's active concurrence on the goal(s). This may not be easy in all cases, but there should be some explicit personal involvement—want, need, desire—on the child's part. He has to be getting something from the situation. One of the pressing complaints of young people today is that oldsters have set goals too unilaterally or narrowly or thoughtlessly. Unless the child is very young or very handicapped in understanding, his participation in the goal-setting process should be sought.

2. Know your child well, and be aware of what "grabs" him in the sense of what is reinforcing. Many parents allege that their children are not much interested in anything, have no real psychological pulse which can be felt, and are more "turned off" than "turned on." This feeling usually arises in parents not out of factual knowledge (we have never known a child wholly adamant against all approaches), but out of poor observational and tactical approaches to the child. One must be ingenious in devising and applying reinforcements.

3. Set up "contracts" with the child, if he is old enough to understand them and if agreements are too involved to keep informal. Schools are beginning to set up contractual agreements with students as part of a motivational (and reinforcement) procedure in regard to academic as well as social and behavioral tasks. These contracts specify what is to be done, by what time (or at what rate), what the "value" of the completed work is in terms of grades, privileges, even money. For example, a given contract might call for the child to mow the lawn at least once a week all summer, for such-and-such pay. Payment for maintaining the lawn mower, providing gas, and the like, must also be specified. With school, the child may contract with his teacher to complete a specified number of problems daily (to a given level of correctness), before he can get "free time off" or engage in some other valued activity in the school. Contracts involving a number of courses in juxtaposition to each other—minimal work to be completed in one course before better-liked work in another course can be added to the child's program (as, arithmetic before music or English before science, if this sequence reverses his preferences)—have also been used to produce educational balance for the child. Once adopted, there are many ways in which contracting as a general educational procedure can be followed, and its adaptability to the home is also promising, though not as well developed.

4. Words can be very effective in controlling behavior, if there is a precedent set by the parent that words mean something; if, that is, the parent means what he says. This is true for promises, contracts, disciplinary actions, praise, and communication in general. The child has to trust the parent; words can be a shortcut to action, but they lose their relevance and meaning if there is no solid behavior on the parent's part to back up the words. This means, of course, that once the child understands complex verbal communication, shaping his responses through action does not have to occur. Words can shortcut the process: "You're free to have Johnny come over after you've done all of your arithmetic" can substitute for the deed if the child understands and trusts the words. We said elsewhere that adults tend to over-talk to children; this is very commonly the case, but talking to the point with the child and backing up words with deeds can be an efficient convenience.

5. Let the child go at his own pace. Regardless of parental pressure, a child cannot go at anyone else's pace that is not appropriate for him. However, to recognize at the outset *that the child does his own pacing is very important.* It is much better than later having to adjust expectations downward, or to get into a tangle with the child because you think he is not working hard enough or fast enough. If he sets his pace and works well at it, reinforcements can follow naturally and achievement is set in motion.

6. Recognize that the child "internalizes" his gains, that is, makes them part of himself without your pressure. The child who, after a few months of piano lessons, goes to the piano daily for his practice period without being told to do so has, so to speak, "internalized" (made part of his self-control) this requirement or bit of self-discipline. The *first control usually comes from outside; later, controls become part of the child by virtue of the disciplinary and orderly model set by the parent or teacher. These self-disciplinary items are not initially inside the child, needing only to be released. Rather, they are first outside the child, in the behavior (or expectations) of others who want to teach the child. It is this adult or parental model exhibiting self-discipline (by setting contingencies and reinforcing) that the child learns. Here learning means the child eventually incorporates the model into his own behavior because it is so useful for getting him what he wants. There is a self-contained feedback for the child; he knows he has done well in carrying out his own desires and the desires of others in which he concurs. This tells him he is "on course."*

7. Creativity follows self-discipline. People sometimes criticize the disciplinary procedures as ignoring or thwarting creativity. But creativity occurs only when one is free to create, and one is free only when he has some mastery of and comfort in his behavior. In art, music, handicrafts, children rise to creativity when they have skills under control that they can innovate from. One does not jump all at once to creativity; one gets there, usually, by small steps and by persistence. The child will not necessarily be creative just because he works hard or is self-disciplined. But the latter will not harm creativity, and will surely enhance its products.

8. Attitudes can be stabilized through the disciplined approach. Many parents ask, "What should we do about attitudes?" The answer is that attitudes are behavior—attitudes are tendencies to think-feel-act in given ways under some set of circumstances. A parent objects, "All right, you teach him to do his arithmetic, or to practice piano, or to do his chores, but that doesn't mean he will like them, that doesn't mean his attitude will change." Part of the answer is that attitudes (expressed opinions, tendencies to act) do change as the child encounters the requirement in question (practicing, doing chores or lessons), learns to do it, and comes to like, appreciate, and feel comfortable with this requirement, as he succeeds with it *and gains reinforcement. He certainly won't learn to like it (or, more important, deal with it constructively) unless he encounters and succeeds with it. Another part of the answer is that he still has to do a number of things—all of us do—despite the fact that we may not relish the activity. If one doesn't like to change a flat tire on his car, he can (if convenient) get someone else to do it for him; but if he is caught out on the road without recourse, he has to change his flat tire whether he likes to or not. Everything we do is not going to be liked; we are all entitled to our preferences. The object of child-rearing—self-discipline and self-control—cannot be to produce people who like everything they do, but to separate the conditions and circumstances of liking to do and having to do, and managing the consequences as well as can be.*

The techniques described in this chapter are designed to help children to develop their self-control and self-discipline. Not everything will work for everyone. The parent or teacher who dislikes the child, for example, may not be able to apply effectively certain techniques, or may apply them punitively. The manner of application—the attitude (which is to say, other aspects of the person's behavior toward the child)—will show through. A piano teacher may be an expert musician herself, but if the teacher's attitude toward the child is "How can you play so poorly?" this will tend to dominate, or at least detract from, other considerations in the teacher-pupil relationship and reduce the effect of reinforcement. In such a case, the teacher would really not be following the principles as stated but would be letting her hostile attitude distort the teaching process.

CHAPTER VIII

Relationships In and Out of the Family

HANDLING RELATIONSHIPS WITHIN the family is one of the most demanding tasks the parent has, especially in these times and most particularly with adolescents. Maintaining discipline within the family with youth of this age is usually difficult, and sometimes the best that the parent can do is to hold on, maintain some kind of communication, and try to exhibit the values and attitudes that he believes are best for the child. If parental values do not seem to take root now, they may nevertheless exercise some long-range effect—sometimes more apparent to an outsider than to the parent directly involved—or at least the values may show in a few years when the youth's intense struggle to be unique relaxes a little and he demonstrates previously dormant habits of attitude and behavior which the parent taught some years earlier.

Often, though, the apparent intractability is more "bark" than "bite," and some shifting on the parent's part can ameliorate the situation considerably. The thrust must always be *positive*, even if the outcome is less hopeful than one wants.

Children at very early ages have always gone through periods of what has been called "negativism," when they automatically say, "No, I don't wanna," to almost anything the parent proposes. Then, as they became adolescent, they have usually turned more strongly, ingeniously, and complexly rebellious. Sometimes this is manifested in overt behavior, such as running away (briefly) from home, physically striking back at the parent, locking themselves in their room, destroying household articles, refusing to eat or participate in family affairs, playing truant from school. The early "negativism" (which is *not* a good word for it) is, however, born differently from later obstinancy. The young child is first separating himself from others and from the animate and inanimate world. Observing his behavior, one can see that, despite negative instances, the young child *is* moving toward and with others to a very great extent.

Rebelliousness Today

Parents who believe that children are more rebellious or more spoiled than ever before in our national history, who have constructed a stereotype in their minds of themselves and their friends as models of good deportment or of at least controlled, respectful behavior toward their elders, are probably forgetting many examples of similar (though it now seems, milder) delinquencies—such as stealing apples, beating up strangers, carving up desks, and writing on walls. They may also be assuming that underneath the rebelliousness they always really did remain respectful of their elders—and do not credit their children now with having the same kind of respect underneath but not showing it. We tend to forget our own shortcomings.

We believe that it is not the fact that rebelliousness exists that marks our children today as different, or even, likely, the intensity of their rebellious attitudes. We cannot establish that our children, with these attitudes, are any different from our generation or past generations of children.

We do believe, however—and this is too obvious to need detailing—that some modes of rebelliousness have changed, and that these forms today perhaps threaten the older generation more because of their especially family disrupting (moving away), socially destructive (dropping out), and personally damaging (drug abuse) nature.

The rebelliousness of youth today has far more dramatic outlets, with far larger effects upon the youth, his family, and society, than ever before. In a past generation, a fourteen-year-old who threatened to run away from home usually had no place to go and ended up returning home lonely and afraid after an hour, day, or week, or was picked up by the police or turned in by a friend or stranger. Today he can run away, find refuge with others of his kind, and be ignored by police and strangers, lost in the massive movement of others like himself. He can, in other words, *get away with it* without apprehension, punishment, or uncertainty—and forces leading to family disruption are increased, no matter how good the intentions or even the training and leadership methods of the parents.

The socially destructive effect comes both in the curtailment of a youth's powers and in the consequent reduction of his contribution to society. While youth is idealistically concerned about the cynicism, selfishness, shortsightedness, and hypocrisy of its elders, it struggles futilely to find effective modes to improve society. While it flounders, it wastes its talents and powers in primitive activities of less developed man—living without tools and goods, tilling the soil, seeking an education solely from observing nature and his fellowman firsthand (and rejecting the additional learning of scholars of past ages).

Personally damaging consequences of current rebelliousness are more easily established and less debatable than the other effects. The dramatic increases in drug use (other than "medicine"), venereal disease, and problems deriving from voluntarily living in poverty attest to destructive consequences of loosened family controls and the exposure of immature human beings to these dangers in the environment that parents protected them from more effectively in past generations.

Drugs have always been available to past generations of youth, in some respects more easily—before 1937, for example, when marijuana was not banned in federal law, and before 1914 when narcotics were not illegal, and before 1919, when alcohol was not barred to children. What is mainly different now, however, is that psychodelic drugs have come into widespread use because they are sought after to fulfill a need of youths escaped from their homes and families with nothing to do that appears to be meaningful. They then ascribe meaning to drug experiences as if that were an adequate substitute for the more conventional activities of education and work that they have been allowed to flee. They also have freedom to indulge in the sheer thrill and immediate gratification related to experimentation and risk-taking.

Our youth, then, has escaped from the confinement in which parents and society traditionally held them, but like zoo animals let loose—or domesticated dogs and cats—they no longer know how (if, genetically, they once did) to fend for themselves in the unfamiliar jungle they escape to.

But even after acknowledging what is perhaps the most trying and challenging rebellion of youth for some generations, we propose the same methods as in other chapters for handling family problems with children and youth. One must, as with any other problems, set goals and work to accomplish them as well as possible, experimenting with any reasonable methods in the forms, with the follow-up and indicated modifications, as suggested in previous chapters.

If *new* forms are to be found to cope with children's and youth's problems beyond the pattern we are suggesting, at least within the foreseeable future, we believe they will come from outside of rather than from within the family. They will come from new forms of social planning and structure. Perhaps children and youth who run away, for example, can be intercepted somewhere, anywhere, in some way, anyway, that will join them together in some substitute for the family, and some substitute for parents—in a way that will hold them for some new form of education and training for different but self-fulfilling and socially useful kinds of work and living. Thus a new chapter in social control and education may be written.

Meanwhile parents are confronted with the need to maintain as effective control and training within the family as they can, for as long as they can, up to the point, at 18 or so, when their children should have been sufficiently educated and trained so that they can leave home and sustain themselves independently, and do so, unless they are pursuing higher education or professional training.

Maintaining Communication

Parents often become desperate about their seeming ineffectiveness with their children. They become more and more frantic in their efforts to achieve a certain result or even simply to hold the child's attention. And finally they may just give up and cut communication with the child. When this occurs in adolescence or later, communication may be cut for months, even years. Or, if maintained, it may be so infrequent and with such a sense of hopelessness on the parent's part, that the contacts have no bite, and the parent makes not even a pretence of expecting to have any effect on the child. These superficial parent-child contacts, following estrangement, seem more to reinforce the adolescent's or youth's negativism than to point the way for more effective ways of communication.

But one stricture at least seems universally appropriate to any discussion of problems within the family. It is that communication should *always* be maintained, at almost any cost in effort and patience—that it should never be cut, or not for long. It may very well be good in an intense conflict situation to quit talking for a little while, to let wounds heal a bit and to cool off before pursuing a problem, but it is not advisable to do this for longer than a few hours. It may not be wise—or necessary—to resume discussion about the point of conflict, it is better to try for a new "beachhead" in such cases. In any event, the parent should never cut off all communication for very long.

The parent may feel that whenever he starts a discussion with the child and no matter what it is about, they will end up fighting and with both feeling bitter and futile about talking at all. And it may well be that matters do go this way between them. But they need not, if the parent can recognize that he is at least as responsible as the child is for how things develop between them. Just as the good classroom teacher learns how to get along with almost all of his students, the good parent learns how to handle each of his children.

He does not *demand* this or that of the child by way of respect or obedience, but rather gives his attention to *how* he can best elicit this or that from the child. If he demands and fails, he then feels angry, bitter, or severely disappointed because he has laid his dignity and status on the line and been rebuffed, and how does he proceed from there? If, on the other hand, he merely tries to move the child to do this or that, in this direction or that, and fails, he can then simply try some other way. It is just a failure of the methods he has used, rather than being a *personal* failure of his own as a parent.

There is yet in our society no adequate substitute for the family. If you as a parent fail to exercise or even to try to exercise effective direction of your child, the chances are that the next forces he will be exposed to will be even less successful. You have nothing to gain and much to lose by breaking off communication with your child, no matter how rebellious he may be. He can always break off with you, if in no other way than simply by leaving home. As long as he does not take that initiative, he is at least physically accessible to any efforts you may extend to try to train him. You should never cease trying to take advantage of that fact.

The Parents' and Children's Roles

We have already described the parental role as that of a teacher. We do not, then, subscribe to the view that the family should be a perfect democracy of equals, children and parents lumped together with one vote each and otherwise with equal powers of determining policy and action, or with each family member the equal of every other in being given, even temporarily, the power to direct.

This does *not* mean that the parent runs the family with an iron hand—even if he could—in a country and society as strongly committed to democratic principles as ours. It does *not* mean that children should have no powerful voice in family decisions or in relations with their parents. It does mean, simply, that the parent, like the teacher in the classroom, has a job to perform in the training of the young, and needs to lead and direct the young with his generally superior experience, judgment, and strength. At least he should try to live up to these potentials as a parent.

Children need not like or willingly accept such a parental role. Do the young of any species? Is the question even relevant on important questions of survival? Indeed, recalcitrance probably characterizes the learning process among all the young throughout the animal world, and a gentle cuffing often occurs to bring the child to attention and conformity with some practice being taught.

What role, then, should children have in relation to parents? It should, we propose, first of all, be that of any learner to a tutor. That is, what needs to be taught, and what must be learned, for survival and effective functioning should have highest priority—as previously discussed. Then, after survival and effective functioning, come values which may be best taught by given special attention to relations within the family and democratic procedures.

Some readers may continue to be concerned that democratic procedures and other values are not put first. We will not here repeat the arguments already discussed which go to the heart of our views on training for self-discipline and competence. We do not depreciate the importance of children's having a strong voice in family policies and actions that affect them. We merely do not want it to occur at the expense of their physical and psychological survival, and the development of their powers.

As far as values are concerned, these do not arise from nowhere. The parent is as much a teacher of values as of skills and self-discipline, and the child is probably no more likely to generate the first for himself than the last two. Some few children, left entirely alone, probably would develop a strong and good set of values to guide their lives, but the larger number probably would drift and experiment for an unnecessarily long time, sifting through their aimless experiences for values that a capable tutor could help them to find and screen. Parents, like other teachers, can be a priceless repository of the experience and wisdom of our civilization. Despite their deficiencies, they are not likely to produce as many seriously defective adults as an entirely undirected, untutored environment would.

When to Interfere

Much parental training is negative. For every time the parent says "Look, dear, please do this" or "Try to do it this way," he probably says five or ten times "Don't do that" or "Don't do it like that," without providing effective positive tutoring. Think, too, of how practical we are with young children, petting and coddling and socially reinforcing them with each developmental gain, and how stingy we are in praise with older children who probably need it more—since alternatives and defeats are more common for them.

Partly the problem for the parent is accepting the role described in the previous section, and in giving it highest priority. If the parent does not see himself primarily as a teacher of his children, or if he puts other goals ahead of it, such as doing personal reading in quiet or acquiring material goods, then he may very well try to achieve his own peace, or time and energy to make money, at the expense of his role as a trainer of his children. To the extent, however, that he wants to train his children effectively, he must give sensitive attention to the goals and success of his training.

With this view firmly in the forefront of his mind, the parent will develop the habit of asking himself, "What do I want my child to do, not alone right now, but as a future habit, and for his best welfare?" He will not have to say these words to himself forever, but he will have to until his behavior with his child *changes* to what he wants it to be.

For change is the key to training. We are trying to change the child's behavior—from nothing to something or from one thing to another. And we are trying to get him to change not only for the moment and for our convenience but, more importantly, for a long time and for his own success and satisfaction.

The change process begins with *interference*. To change behavior, the parent must interfere with what is going on that should be done differently, whether because of a lack of behavior, ineffectual behavior, or self-defeating behavior—to bring about behavior that will be more effective in reaching the desired goals.

But when should the parent interfere? Two limitations appear to be desirable. He should not interfere when the child, in fairly efficient and not damaging ways, seems likely to find a satisfactory solution or course of action for himself. And he should not interfere in matters too trivial to matter much to the child's future. In the first case our assumption is that, *other circumstances being equal,* it is perhaps somewhat better for the child to find his own solutions—even though it is probably the *reward* inherent in the solution rather than who finds it, and how, that means most for learning. In the second instance, the parent should conserve his energy and impact for important problems, since if he treats all problems as if they were of equal significance, he fritters away his effect on the child and does not help the child to learn to distinguish, and concentrate on, important matters.

The parent *should* interfere, then, we believe, when the child is not likely to find his own solutions, or is likely to be damaged by the process, or will find solutions so circuitously that he will waste much time and energy that could be better used. And he should interfere on matters of the most vital importance to the child's future, where the parent's usually superior judgment and experience will add to the child's competence even if the child could find some solution for himself.

We will discuss in Part III the possible solutions of various problems the parent encounters. Here we want to deal primarily with relationships and roles between parent and child. The matter of when to interfere in the child's affairs is a particularly sensitive one because, in large part, it sets the tone of the relationship. The nosy parent, the nagging parent, the aloof parent, the indifferent parent, the picky parent, the negative parent, all, as their labels indicate, are showing a mistiming or misdirection in their interference with the child's behavior.

In most of these cases, the parent is *not* acting on any clear set of goals that he has chosen, nor any clear set of principles governing how and when he should interfere. He is acting largely or entirely on the basis of his own habitual behavior, derived from his own needs and frustrations. He *wants* to help his child, he *hopes* to guide his child's behavior toward success—but he does not know or take time to analyze *how* to do so most effectively.

When to interfere, then, should be determined by the parent's evaluation of the importance of the problem and of the necessity or desirability of intervention. It should also be affected by an ability to document to the child that there is a problem which affects or will affect the child more than the parent, by the parent's capability to help with a solution and not merely to complain, by a sincere and continuing interest on the part of the parent and not merely a passing or superficial concern.

These suggestions about when the parent should intefere are designed to help him become as effective as possible *and* to establish a good relationship with the child. These two objectives are not identical, however. While a good relationship usually enhances the training and educational process, and is itself aided when the parent is effective, a good relationship is not necessary for effective training. It cannot be depended upon to develop even if the parent is as good a parent as possible from the standpoint either of training *or* catering to the child.

His desire to raise his child well should be founded in love, and he should cultivate loving feelings in himself and the child, as a highly valued human feeling and social good. But the decision about when to interfere in the child's life can and should be based, like most decisions discussed throughout this book, upon what will produce the best effect in the child. Love sets the stage for parent-child interaction, but it does not tell the participants how best to proceed to reach their goals.

The parent's decision about when to interfere in the child's life, then, should not be made with an eye to whether the child will probably like or not like the parent as a consequence of the interference. In the long run and most deeply, the child's love for the parent will not be based, any more than the parent's love for the child, on a parent's interference in his life, for his own long-run benefit.

How many older children and adults have complained bitterly that their parents were too easy on them, let them get by with this or that, did not *insist* they work at certain tasks or acquire certain skills! Is there not at least one such youth or adult for every one who complains of a too demanding or interfering parent? And are there not at least as many youths and adults who brag of the love illustrated by the strong intervention of their parents in their lives as there are those who speak regretfully of the parent who left them alone to develop as they wished?

How to Interfere

The most important issues concerning how to interfere have to do with the principles of learning and training discussed elsewhere—goals, priorities, structure for change, experimentation, follow-up, modification. Here we would discuss the relationship between parent and child as the parent goes about intervening in the child's life.

Perhaps most important is that the parent prepare himself to intervene on the basis of the child's welfare and not, primarily, for his own convenience—and that, after he has established this attitude clearly and firmly in his own mind, he translate it into behavior with his child.

This may be the most difficult part of the entire process for the parent, and we do not mean to imply that it can be achieved easily or quickly. But by reminding himself frequently of this view, discussing it often with his or her spouse and others, and bringing it up with the child who is encouraged to object to any inconsistencies and contradictions he notices, the parent can in time move toward this goal. He may never completely succeed in his aim, and he must accept the inevitability of successive approximations, small steps, and some setbacks.

But the parent can hold out to himself large personal rewards for some sacrifices of personal comforts in favor of training his child: he can reap great satisfaction from having reared a child to competent adulthood. Success is, of course, uncertain, and expressed appreciation unlikely, but if the enterprise of raising children is undertaken at all, it should, as with any other large enterprise, be done as well as possible with a maximum effort to succeed.

What is a life-and-death enterprise to the child should at least be very important, serious, and well-considered to the parent. How he interferes, then, in the child's life should be characterized by an earnestness that transmits itself to the child.

In tone, he should interfere with a sense of strength but not arrogance in his superior role, due to his experience and judgment. We use these words frequently about the parent's role with the child, recognizing that many parents have weaknesses in these regards, and that their children may outstrip them in any of these respects before they leave home. Nevertheless, the parent who tries hard to train his child well will almost always, we believe, be able to contribute substantially to the child's welfare through-out the training period—even if the child is rebellious and unappreciative and shows no immediate results of the training.

The parent should interfere in *positive* and *kind* ways, setting gainful alternatives and whenever possible avoiding punishing methods. Putting aside human considerations for the moment, though we should always give them high priority, present evidence is that positive methods are more effective than negative ones—except, perhaps, with severely disturbed persons or for immediate effect, as when a child runs into the street.

This is not to say that painful or unkind methods should never be used. Just as a shot in the arm or drilling on teeth may be necessary for the child's physical health, so a sharp slap, the loss of a pet or money because of carelessness or mistreatment, or the withholding of an allowance or a treasured television show because an assigned task has not been performed may be necessary or desirable for his psychological development. Painful or temporarily cruel methods should never deliberately be chosen if alternatives are available, but neither should they be avoided when necessary for safety or important training situations.

There should be open and direct interaction between parent and child, in part so that the child is being taught to assert himself effectively in relation to his elders, and in part so that the parent has a chance to profit from feedback from the child. By speaking up and having his views respected, the child opens himself up to the opportunity to learn how to interact well, without necessarily gaining his way. But the parent also can and should learn from the child. By encouraging the child to speak up, listening to him, and adapting to his views when they have merit, the parent can correct or modify his own attitudes and methods. When the child does not speak, he can neither improve his effectiveness with the parent nor help the parent to improve his effectiveness with the child. The parent should seldom aim at silencing the child, but should provide direction.

Extent of Control

To what extent should the parent exercise control in the family? When and how he should intervene has already been discussed, but how firm and extensive should his control be? Should the other children in the family be enlisted to support the parental objectives with any one child, and should children and adults outside of the home also be used?

A balance needs to be found between the most explicit and powerful training methods, which tend to maximize control—that is, be operating all the time, utilizing all of the environment as much as possible—and the subtle harmony and effectiveness of the family unit and family relationships as well as relationships outside of the family. The latter may be a stronger educational force in the long run.

The parent must give attention not only to his effectiveness as a trainer of one child, but also to his role as co-head of a family unit, as teacher of the other children in the family, and as coordinator of family relationships with neighbors, friends, and school.

There is no essential incompatability, of course, between training children alone and training in relationship to other children and adults. Both are necessary. But the parent cannot, indeed should not, attempt to exercise as much control over the child's behavior outside of the home as within it.

For one thing, he cannot; his opportunities to observe and guide the child are more limited outside the home. For another, it is desirable for the child to be exposed to other influences and sources of control. He will be guided or trained in his life by many others besides his parents: other children, relatives and adult friends, ministers, youth leaders, athletic coaches, employers, policemen, school counselors, physicians. The parent, however, is the master teacher, and he is in position to control to some extent the kind of other influences to which the child will be exposed. And, we believe, he should exercise this prerogative.

But having directed or permitted his child's exposure to these other influences, he must be prepared to allow their interplay with the child. He is doomed to constant worry, friction, and frustration if he tries to control not only the general areas of influence to which his child is exposed but also the exact nature of all influences.

Coordination With Influences Outside the Home

The parent should not ignore the child's activities outside the home. Effective training must include consideration and inclusion of influences throughout the child's environment, and the parent can affect the nature of such influences. The principles of training outside the home are the same as in the home, but the parent's role is less reliable and less intense, and is one step removed from direct influence. It is at best a position of master coordinator.

To the extent it is successful, that is, it is a role of master coordination of forces outside the home. Because it is indirect, control is diluted and success is even less certain than when training is direct. The balance here is even more sensitive between what can and cannot be done and, therefore, between what should and should not be attempted. There is no use, for example, for you, the parent, to try to control all friendships your child may form. You simply cannot possibly exercise control over his relationships with all the children he may meet and like and cultivate, or who may cultivate him, in school, on the playground, in the neighborhood, at club meetings, or in other homes.

You attempt, then, to do only what you have a reasonable chance to succeed with. You try to influence him to visit certain groups, homes, clubs, activities that you think best for him—leaving yourself always open to growth in yourself from information about new places and people that he or others may tell you about. You try to train him in a sense of values, and judgment, that will make discrimination and good decisions on his part more likely. You keep yourself as well-informed as you can without snooping, and preferably through open and friendly conversation with your child on his activities outside the home. You intervene in his outside activities, but only on those rare occasions when you think he is endangered by them, physically or psychologically, or when they are having a disruptive effect on his life in ways you consider of highest importance—in his use of drugs, in his association with a group that is, say, shoplifting, or in his staying out late at night and not getting his schoolwork or household tasks done.

As far as worrying about "bad influences" on your child is concerned—perhaps children whose behavior you do not approve of, or homes and other parents with habits and attitudes which are disturbing or displeasing to you—you cannot, of course, shield your child from all such influences. In fact, Grandma or Aunt Kate may be the worst influence of all, yet you do not even consider trying to keep your child away from them.

So you do what you can, intervening only when it seems essential for a specific and important purpose, hoping that you can train your child well in how to handle adverse situations. Occasionally, also, you may try to intervene with other children and parents to get them to modify their behavior, particularly as it affects your child. But considering how difficult and uncertain your efforts are to control situations under your nose, you must adapt to the fact that the influence you can exercise on those with whom you have no important accepted role is almost certain to be weak and ineffectual unless circumstances are unusually favorable.

Rather than trying to change others outside the home, you may instead be able to enlist their help in specific ways directed at your child. Another parent may be willing, for example, to insist that your child leave his friend's home by nine P.M., or other youths may be willing to come to your home to meet or play together where you can at least observe what goes on, or a youth leader may be willing, at your request, to assign your son or daughter to an activity you think would be valuable.

Your most effective role, then, with those who influence your child outside the home is not to train them for your purpose, but rather to coordinate influences on your child outside of your home. Without trying to control his outside affairs—you should prefer to train him in how to handle them well by himself—you can be alert to what is going on, using your information mainly to help him to solve outside problems himself, but occasionally also to intervene directly or indirectly for a specific limited purpose.

Feelings Within the Family

So far we have tried to keep our suggestions about training as direct and specific as possible. We recognize, however, that there are many emotional complications to our viewpoint and to the suggestions we make. We have written other books that deal specifically with emotional problems and their treatment, and we do not intend to comment in detail on the subject here.

Certain primarily emotional problems do, however, intrude in a practical way in this educational process. We will discuss them from time to time, but only those that directly affect the training procedures we are describing. For example, although you as one parent in the family are presumably personally interested enough to read this book and perhaps try out its views and suggestions, your spouse, the other parent in the family, may not want to do so, may disagree with the viewpoint and methods, and may fight against any implementation you may wish to try. One or more of your children may take similar exceptions.

Assuming that you are having problems in training your children along the lines that this book discusses, and that you are not making enough progress with them to satisfy your spouse and you, rationally you and your spouse should be willing to try any method within reason that gives hope of working. You should not reject it out of hand, without any experience with it, merely because of some preconceived notions or prejudices.

But if your spouse does not agree and does not want to cooperate, you can still try, within the limits of your influence in the family and your direct relationship with your child, to intervene with the child's behavior that is subject to your control. If, for example, you as the father are or could be the one who pays a weekly allowance, you can announce that the allowance will be paid only after performance of certain tasks. Hopefully your wife will have agreed on this approach and will cooperate by helping to design the tasks and to check on their accomplishment. But if she is unwilling to, but has no better proposal for getting the child to do his tasks, then you can proceed anyway—provided only that she agrees not to sabotage your efforts in such ways as giving the child money upon request or discouraging his work.

Similarly you, as mother, may want to require that the child complete her homework or do the dishes before she can look at her favorite television program, but your husband may not want to be so "hard" on the child, and say, "What's the difference, before or after? It means so much to her to watch the show!" Provided he does not actually undercut you, you can proceed to try out the approach anyway, and hope that, if it is successful, your husband will come to appreciate, accept, and cooperate with it.

As far as the children are concerned, they are likely to balk at the institution of any more vigorous or disciplined procedures than they are used to. But if and as successes are produced, they, above all others involved, will profit from them. They will gain a sense of personal competence, power, and satisfaction—as well as whatever external rewards are provided—and these are, after all, the measure of the success of the approach. The children are not in a position or of a proper mind to judge such methods in advance. They lack what the method is intended to provide. They can only judge in retrospect.

The children can and should be asked for their reactions and opinions continually, however, for it is the impact on them, even though it is the long-term rather than the immediate one, that is the measure of our efforts. We should therefore be sensitive to their reactions and continually make modifications in our methods accordingly. But the long-term forward-looking plan must always come from the parents.

CHAPTER IX

Learning Social Living

THERE ARE MANY paths children can take for social living. Unfortunately many parents have a single goal in mind: encouraging, nagging, bullying, persuading, reinforcing their children to become as popular, approval-seeking, gregarious, extroverted as possible. And many of the children of such parents respond by becoming rebellious and defensive, seeking their own more selective and limited companionship—or going through life like zombies being pushed about by the whims of others whose approval they think is necessary for the happiness which they never find. Often parents really know but fail to accept and teach their children that the popularity they seek but seldom achieve is shallow and flimsy and never does provide them with inner security.

If parents would consult their own experiences and feelings directly and honestly, many would have to admit that they have never felt satisfaction or tranquility for long by courting popularity and the approval of others. Yet they may blindly impose this goal on their children—mainly, perhaps, because they do not know a better way or, indeed, may never have considered the merit of alternative ways. Most people who claim to have found satisfaction in their relations with others seem to have found it through cultivating close ties with a very few people, through depending upon their own mind and senses so that they try primarily to please themselves and not others, through finding resources in themselves, supplemented, perhaps, by those of a very few, close others at times of problems or crises.

But these perhaps are the extremes of adjustment one can make in dealing with others to gain greatest satisfaction. One can move to any degree in either direction, and with variations. Furthermore, there are many different general approaches in our culture and in others, such as that of teacher or disciple, of self-abnegation, of hermitism, of martyrdom, of wanderlust, of hedonism, of powerseeking, of conflict.

No single one of these roles seems to satisfy most men, however, and we are here seeking guidelines that can be most universally useful. Obviously, we believe that goals for social living must be found before the parent can help train his child in this area. What shall they be? Shall they include successful extroversion—or introversion? Popularity—or self-sufficiency? Effective independence—or dependence? Selfish satisfaction—or unselfishness? Or what?

Even though we believe that there are some goals that are more likely than others to yield more personal satisfaction more of the time for most people, and that such goals derive from one's values and philosophy, we also believe that social goals should be, whenever and as soon as possible, personally chosen by the child (except where serious social or personal damage is likely to result).

There are universal goals which we have already discussed, universal for clear reasons of personal and social survival. Beyond those, however, the goals of social living can and should, we believe, be left up to the persons involved. Meanwhile, however, parents have much they can teach their children by way of *social competence* and by way of *alternative values* in social living. Parents will, of course, have their own tastes in social living and their own modes of social behavior, and they cannot help but influence their children with their example alone. Nor can they curb entirely their tendency to shape their children with their beliefs that popularity, independence, outspokenness, creativity, secretiveness, or whatever, are virtues to be cultivated. Nor is it possible to succeed, even when one wants and tries hard, *not* to influence a child toward what one believes.

We suggest that the parent avoid training the child in a particular mode of social living (with the exceptions suggested above), but primarily concentrate on teaching the major *social skills*, so that the child can choose and do well with any mode he may eventually prefer. Whatever the child's gradually developing personal tastes lead him to—introversion or extroversion, openness or reticence, creativity or restraint, independence or dependence—the mode should be his own and, if possible, be respected by the parent.

What Are "Alternative Values"?

The larger part of this chapter will be concerned with social skills, rather than values. This is not because we do not consider social values to be extremely important, but rather because we believe that children should, as far as possible, choose them for themselves, Besides, we have little faith that parents can teach values *other than their own*, or can curb their tendency to teach their own. Because we hope for better values in the younger generation than in ours, and because we also believe that people should choose their own values as the most precious option in their lives, we recommend a light parental hand in this area, and concentration only on the "universals"—and on presentation of a wide range of alternatives.

Despite these limitations, parents will inevitably, through word and deed, teach their own values (though word and deed may differ), as poorly developed and confused as they may be. Parents can, of course, try to clarify and develop their values, but how to do so cannot be covered here. Suffice it to say now that this would be a most worthy enterprise. And parents can try to present a tolerant and informed attitude toward values with which they do not agree (but do not consider harmful or dangerous).

Such acceptable "alternative values" which the child may well choose for himself regardless of his parents' attitudes might well include preference for relatively social or relatively individual activity; preference for openness in revealing himself, or for reticence; preference for service to others, or for development of more personal skills; preference for relative independence of others, or for interdependency relationships. Thousands of other "alternative values" might be listed. These are merely among the most common, and the least subject to agreement in a principled way. That is, whether a person chooses to lead a highly social or relatively lonely life, or whether he chooses to serve others or create for himself, need concern no one but him (unlike honesty versus dishonesty, or fair play versus bullying).

Is there clearly a special validity to one or the other alternative in each of these pairs? We think not. It would be an unfortunate imposition on the child if the parent insisted on one or the other and imparted a sense of guilt to the child who disagreed, as if only the parent's value were correct. The child could then only slowly and painfully modify his attitude if he later decided the value was not his preference.

Where values are as uncertain as here, the parent can encourage an experimental, open-minded attitude by the child, to try out, judge, and decide for himself among the possibilities open to him. The parent can help train him in flexibility and open-mindedness, and to endure uncertainty and indecision when it is in the good cause of growing until finally a decision can be derived, when necessary, founded upon as full information and experience as possible.

What Are Social Skills?

Mainly, however, we would have parents teach social skills, specific and general, that will permit the child to take care of himself well, to gain the *resources* to choose and live with whatever values he prefers, and to possess the *methods* to choose his way of life and be able to live it satisfyingly. Thus equipped, he will be able to select his values wisely and progressively, as he matures. With his knowledge, skills, and self-discipline as highly developed as possible, he has open to him a wider range of options among modes of life than if he is left to flounder.

What, then, are the social skills, the areas of competence, which will maximize the child's opportunities to choose among the widest variety of ways of life for one that will suit him best? The major areas would seem to be *educational, vocational, financial, companionable,* and *sexual.*

Unless the child can be trained to handle these areas of his life competently, not only does he severely limit his opportunities to choose a way of life, but he may very well be caught up in a web of trouble to such an extent that he must struggle simply to survive and to meet his most elemental needs, and have no time or energy left to seek out the finer aspects of existence. For example, if he cannot carry through the training necessary to earn a living in an area of his interest and ability, he may have to work at simple labor that totally uses him up, just to earn his food and shelter. Or if he has a sexual hunger that is continually unsatisfied because he is afraid to meet women or is ineffective with them, his constant thinking about sex may consume his energies and distract him from developing himself in other areas.

We suggest, then, that the parent's major task in preparing the child for satisfying social living should be to try to give him the knowledge, skills, and self-discipline that will open the widest range of options to him on the basis of his developing abilities, interests, values. The major areas for attention—the educational, vocational, financial, companionable, sexual—should then be the subject of training between parent and child.

Educational Skills

Educational skills will be discussed in Chapters X and XI. Here we will merely comment on their importance for increasing the child's range of choices in his social world.

The child must master elementary levels of education in order to transact the simplest functions in his world—to take transportation, to make change, to read the news that may affect him, to correspond with those important in his life. Satisfying social living, indeed survival, will depend upon his mastering such transactions. Otherwise he may need to live his life under the protection of a guardian or an institution—or take a chance on being frequently cheated, for example, or unable to get to a desired destination, or losing touch with those dear to him.

Higher education will have less to do with survival and more to do with satisfying his curiosity about the world, giving him skills in language, culture, current history, social relations, human behavior, or whatever else will permit him to extend the complexity and pleasures of his life. Higher education also will provide the basis for the most complex, highest-level, and most remunerative work he is capable of. It is likely to provide the most satisfying and efficient (most money for least time) way to make his living.

How the parent can contribute best to this process will

be discussed in subsequent chapters. The importance of this process to the child's satisfaction with his social living is what we would establish here.

Vocational Skills

The need for vocational skills is often ignored or given only secondary attention in American homes. True, many parents and relatives ask children from a young age, "What are you going to be when you grow up?" And some parents press their high-school-age youngsters to decide on a profession. Many parents, perhaps most, pressure their children to go to college so that they can better prepare themselves for a high level of work and make "good money."

This approach shares nothing, however, with the consistent, reasoned, careful, and long-pursued course of interest and activity that leads to the wise choice of an occupation, a training program for it, personal satisfaction with it, and changes from it when clearly desirable.

A good deal more thoughtful and consistent attention should be given to the way the child will earn his living and spend the largest block of his waking hours when an adult. How he makes his living will, in fact, determine how he lives much of the rest of his life. How, then, can the parent help most to see that his child finds satisfaction when he must earn his own living?

When the child is between five and ten, the parent can give special attention to his interests, abilities, and talents, and not only encourage him by words and deeds (such as taking him to relevant exhibits, shows, movies) but also by making appropriate materials and classes available to him. The parent can also help the child to master what he is trying to learn, and reward him for his special accomplishments.

At this younger age, it is more important to observe potentialities and provide a wide range of materials and other resources with which the child can experiment than it is to discuss specific occupations. The parent should, meanwhile, be applying the principles of training, self-discipline, and achievement discussed in Part I. For example, in presenting resources to the child so that he can experience the materials and tasks of various occupations, the parent should not *distract* him so that self-discipline and depth of acquaintanceship are impaired. On the contrary, concentration to a reasonable completion point should be encouraged before another type of work is begun. This is very important, for all of us—especially children—are too open to distraction to learn current tasks as well as possible. Concentration and setting short-term goals are very important.

Then, in the age period of perhaps eleven to fifteen, the experimentation and acquaintance with occupations can become more specific and realistic. The youth can be encouraged and helped to work with people employed in fields of his interest. For his vocational future, it is probably better that he work for little or nothing near people in whose field he has interest, than that he earn the best money he can without regard to his interests.

Parents often speak of how desirable it is for children to "learn the value of money," by which they usually mean the hard work involved in earning it as well as the difficulties of deciding how to spend it and paying for what they want. But hard work can be involved whether the money comes from an outside employer or from a parent, and managing it presents the same problems whether it is earned or an allowance.

Thus we make a case for the importance to the child of gaining early vocational experiences which have value for his future planning, as contrasted with work primarily for money. *If* the youth's earnings do crucially help the family's financial condition, surely the work has an importance of high priority. But if it contributes an unneeded amount to the family's coffers or merely reduces the amount of allowance the father needs to provide, it would seem logical to place the vocational value of the adolescent's job above its financial return.

The logic here is exactly the same as that for pursuing formal education. Even though the youth can earn money by dropping out of school prematurely, he will in that way abort his opportunity to grow and to realize his fullest potential occupationally, if he has the ability to master a vocation that requires further formal education.

His formal education during this age period of eleven to fifteen, spanning mainly the junior high school years, will for the first time have clear vocational implications and begin to lay the groundwork for what he will need for specific jobs. But he need not specialize or commit himself in any way, and it would seem ill-advised for teachers, parents, or counselors to try to direct, limit, and focus him toward specific work. This can, with great profit and without commensurate disadvantage, be a period of flexibility and experimentation. The youth can test himself on trades courses, science, mathematics, languages, English skills, social and recreational classes, and whatever else he can fit into his schedule.

Too often, separate educational tracks have already begun to restrict his choice. Yet many supposedly college-bound students can find much value and perhaps a most satisfying kind of work in a trade or manual skill. And students of supposedly limited intelligence may find growing interest in and aptitude for science or language which can mature appropriately with college-level objectives.

Finally, in the high school years—the last years in which the parent is likely to have important influence in the youth's way of life in society, and his occupational course—the parent can perhaps act as a serious observer of his children's interests and aptitudes, aid them to the extent that the parent possesses skills or knowledge beyond his children's in areas of their interests, help them to get valuable work experiences, and provide or put them in touch with resources that will enlarge the range of their choices as well as the depth of their background.

Unless the youth's interests crystallize during this time and his aptitudes are clearly appropriate, there is still no reason to "freeze" an occupational choice. After all, the youth can continue to grow and mature for years to come, and the risk of choosing an occupation poorly would seem to outweigh the advantages of specializing and limiting himself as early as possible. He can keep a wide range of occupational options available to himself usually up to the junior year in college, and he can generally profit by doing so as long as he is learning good work habits and enlarging his educational and work experiences.

In exercising whatever influence he may have with his child during this last period, the parent needs to balance serious attention to the process of choosing an occupation against anxiety about getting set in life. Serious and consistent attention is likely to be of far more value to the son or duaghter than anxiety and pressure. The occupational choice has, after all, at least as far-reaching implications for the youth's life as his choice of a mate and companions or anything else. It should therefore be arrived at as any decision of utmost importance in his life, involving the fullest and richest range of his thinking and feeling, his experience and knowledge.

In all work areas, working habits, reliability, dependability, and follow-through are important. These attitudes and supportive skills can be taught in school or out of school, and especially in the home. Chores, privileges, pay for work contingent upon its quality, all can contribute to work skills necessary for success in any occupation. The parent can do much to aid the child's development in these ways and help build self-respect and self-discipline at the same time.

Financial Skills

Managing money wisely is also a vital part of effective social living. Much more than the simple expenditure of money is involved. How one manages money will affect and be affected by how hard and at what one is required to work, and the priority one gives to material goods generally and to such specific choices as house or car, education or travel, liquor or books, recreation or security, television or smoking, and the kind and amount of each. Regardless of whether one puts it to himself in this way, if one spends money in one way, he cannot spend it in another. A new car may cost as much as a trip to Europe, and one is making a choice between the two, potentially at least, if one purchases either.

Furthermore, there are many practical aspects in the use of money after decisions are made that will affect how much it covers. Is it drawing as much interest as it could, is the purchase of a house or car being done as economically as possible, are the goods which are being bought the longest-lasting and most nearly repair-free that could be chosen? To the extent that purchases are not made wisely, the person may have to give up on a job or change he wants to make, but which pays less. To replace a car, he may have to curtail his education. Or to buy new furniture, the husband or wife may have to take on an extra, exhausting job.

If the parent has the knowledge and skill to teach his children how to manage money wisely, he can improve the effectiveness of their social living substantially, and the satisfaction they can derive from their way of life. If the parent lacks the skills himself (and many do), he can best help his children (as well as himself) by admitting his weaknesses and problems in this area, trying to learn how to overcome them, seeking help from bank counselors or family agencies if necessary, and at least not teaching his children bad habits through his poor example.

The elements of good money management that the parent can try to teach his children involve deciding what one's earning capacity can and will be, given such factors as his abilities and interests, how hard he wants to work and at what, and economic conditions; establishing the general level of expenditure he wants to live at and what kind of living (as with dependents or not) he wants to support; and setting priorities among the items he wants to spend his money on. He would then set up a specific plan of allocating the money according to the income, level of expediture, and priorities. In other words, he would develop a detailed budget that he would hold to except for minor adjustments. Finally, he would follow up on and adjust the budget according to planned changes and practical problems.

Children can be given elementary help in budgeting their money—earned or given as an allowance. Starting with the young child, out of an allowance of perhaps 25 cents he may take a dime (or nickel) to spend immediately, a dime to give for Sunday School (or some other regular payment in keeping with family values), and the rest to defer spending temporarily. As he gets older the amount of money increases, as does the variety of things he can spend money on and the foresight to save for a large item. These choices make up *values*, and they serve as ways to state decisions. The earlier begun, the better.

At all points the child's decisions about his money are, in miniature, a pattern for his future responsibilities, and, as such, are good training in self-discipline and self control.

Companionable Skills

Social skills, to most people, mean the ability to get

along with others, particularly in groups. Often they mean to be popular, to be invited out, to be considered charming, to be given attention by others, and to be able to obtain what you want from others. In this chapter we have defined social skills much more broadly, to include how one gets along in society by way of obtaining what one wants from life. The social skills, in our sense, include the ability to get what you want from your environment that satisfies you most, with respect for others' rights and wants.

The pattern of the child's specific relationships with others, which we hope he will choose and develop for himself, may be almost infinitely varied. Here, however, we want to deal specifically also with the skills required to make friends, to the extent that one wants friends. We assume that the human condition tends to be a lonely one, lonely at least more than most people voluntarily choose to be. But one should be able to learn how to find companions and to make friends when one wants to. That is the skill we refer to here, which the parent should be able to help his children to develop from the earliest age when they begin to meet other children.

We do *not* refer to the parent's desire that her children be popular, or to pressure on the child to put approval from others above all other considerations in his relationships with them. We *do* refer to the child's naturally developing desire for companionship and friends, which often is on a very small scale, much more limited throughout his childhood than the parents may wish. Yet if you ask the average parent how many friends *she* has, it will usually be a far smaller number than she wants for her child.

In any case, our emphasis here is on the child's desire for companionship, and not on the parent's wishes for him. Occasionally a child is extremely withdrawn and the parent is rightfully concerned that he is too fearful of other children, or too passive about seeking them out or doing things with them. But even in such cases, except for outright psychosis, the route the parent can most profitably pursue is the same as for other children without such serious problems.

The best procedure for the parent to follow in any case of undesired loneliness would seem to be that of helping the child to develop skills in making friends and companions *when, as, and to the extent that he wants them.* These skills can be quite clearly seen and fairly well taught—as much as most of the other simpler skills in living.

Perhaps the biggest single obstacle to making friends when one wants them, in both adults and children, is a fear of being rejected or ignored if one makes overtures. To say "hello" to someone, to want him for a friend, and to invite him to do this or that with you, then to have your wishes and efforts ignored or rebuffed—to many people this seems somehow disgraceful, embarrassing, and painful. Instead of considering the effort as a courageous first, perhaps faltering, step in a chain of similar small steps that will almost certainly lead eventually to friendships, those who will be unsuccessful, who will not develop this social skill, will see it as proof of hopeless social incompetence and undesirability. And they will act like burnt children, thereafter avoiding taking the initiative to make friends.

In such cases the parent can make clear to her child that the problem and the first step toward a solution remain the same despite an initial failure. Here is another form of self-discipline, that of learning to persist, to let only natural failure after reasonable efforts over time rather than anxiety dictate whether a different solution should be attempted.

The parent can teach the child much more about how to find companions and make friends. She can, for example, encourage her child to go to places where children of congenial interests are most likely to be found, to develop interest in others and skill in talking with them, to acquire recreational, creative, and other interests and capabilities which others may share, to practice social activities on the assumption that many friendships develop out of shared events rather than initial attraction. And to invite other children to their home.

Emphasis upon the child's felt needs for companionship rather than parental expectations or some imagined social norm can make the child less dependent upon immediate success and more capable of the kind of discipline that will permit friendships to develop slowly, as they usually do.

Many children—and adults—feel rejected by a group, for example, because they are not immediately welcomed, given attention, and asked to participate. They do not realize that this is not generally the way groups function, that the stranger needs slowly to become better known to them before he is likely to be accepted and trusted. This, too, can be taught the child—and also how to elicit feedback from acquaintances that may tell him of his objectionable behavior and how it affects others. And even how to endure loneliness as part of the general human condition when congenial companions are simply not available or accessible, without feeling that you are a miserable failure as a human being.

From the time the baby reacts to the social environment, the individual is developing social skills. The parent has many opportunities to guide and shape these skills. A few examples are:

1. *Giving overt approval to the child when he does well or follows guidance.*

2. *Trying to ignore his small social failures and concentrate on his successes.*

3. *Setting the style for, and complimenting him on, manners at mealtimes, waiting for his turn, sharing toys and equipment with visiting playmates.*

4. *Teaching postponement of gratification—sitting without eating until others have taken their place, eating after the host has begun, offering first place in line to others who may be handicapped.*

5. *Making yourself a model for and encouraging the common social amenities such as expressing appreciation for gifts. Providing* actual practice—*verbally*—*before a child visits another or attends a party.*

We might comment, finally, on what is apparently a changing mode of social behavior in adolescence. What has been discussed so far may be applicable to children up to adolescence rather than later. With older children, parents now seem often to be more concerned (and properly so) about their physical and mental safety in school and on the street, their unconventional and sometimes asocial thinking. Parents may be more anxious about their older children's social activities than their lack of them.

Older adolescents particularly, now, seem to have relatively little trouble finding and relating to groups. They seem to travel about much more and in mixed groups, with girls as parts of gangs as well as boys. This probably makes it much easier than a generation earlier for older children to find companionship and friendships, and results in "popularity" being much less a concern to parents or children.

To the extent this situation exists for her adolescents, the parent's task becomes one of helping her children to establish and maintain their own standards of conduct more than to learn how to relate to others. Self-concepts and self-discipline in such circumstances become all the more important.

Sexual Competence

We have included sexual competence among the several major areas of training for the parent to attend to, in large part because the neglect and distortion of sexual attitudes and behavior in adolescence can so damage, distort, and destroy home and family in adulthood. Indeed, if sexual needs are not satisfactorily attended to they will often determine the course of adult life. Satisfactorily taken care of, sexual needs become a relatively small though pleasurable part of the mature life. It is not the man who has learned to satisfy his sexual (and other) needs as they arise within the ordinary context of his life who is likely to concentrate on sex in his adult life to the extent that it determines his occupation, his geographical location, his social relations, or his recreational activities. It is the youth whose sexual needs are not naturally satisfied as they arise within the total context of his educational, recreational, and social life in whom, as an adult, sex is more likely to become a determining factor—as in many homosexuals, seemingly insatiable and promiscuous adults, or constant thrill-seekers.

We believe, then, that there is good reason for the parent to try to influence her child in his sexual behavior as another form of social living where competence can be learned. Although privacy and personal taste is perhaps most highly developed in this area, the child and youth nevertheless can be well-educated in the facts and attitudes that seem to produce the most satisfying sexual behavior. In addition, the general approach to problem-solving, self-discipline, and achievement which is the theme of this book is as directly applicable to sexual behavior as to any other.

The parent should begin by assuming that there is no question about *whether* her adolescent son or daughter has sexual interests and behavior but that the question is, rather, *what* they are. They can, of course, be left entirely with the child, as a private matter—or entirely to school or companions—if the parent is willing to abandon his or her role as teacher in this particular area and—unlike his or her desire to influence the child's educational, vocational, social, or financial behavior—to leave his education and behavior in regard to sex entirely up to others.

Of course many parents feel ignorant or otherwise uncomfortable in this area. In such cases they may need to educate themselves or get counseling first—which would be valuable directly to themselves and indirectly to their children. Assuming, however, that the parent does have something she can teach the child about sex, she should proceed to do so as early as the child expresses interest, perhaps sooner if the child is generally reluctant to ask questions, and in any case, by age 11 or 12—just before adolescence.

For younger children, giving them a school textbook used for sex education which you have read and approve of, then discussing it with them, is perhaps the best beginning. For older adolescents, perhaps an adult manual, such as *The Art and Science of Love,* * *if* you first read and approve of it, would be the best starting place, followed by conversation about it.

As far as influencing behavior beyond the effect of accurate and complete information, the parent can at best exercise small influence, and then, perhaps, only in the direction of certain attitudes and perspectives—in addition, that is, to the principles of self-discipline and problem-solving discussed elsewhere but also applicable here.

Certain principles of sexual behavior seem to have special value: that sexual needs are normal and should be highly pleasurable; that it is legally safer and socially less restrictive to engage in sex by mutual consent and for mutual pleasure with persons of the opposite sex than in other ways; that such minority practices as homosexuality, nymphomania and satyriasis, sadism, masochism, and fetishism are *not* born in one, that they are learned, that they tend to interfere with other areas of one's life; that

*By Albert Ellis (Dell, 1965).

one need not, indeed probably should not, marry primarily for sexual satisfaction, since that tends to be an insubstantial basis for a permanent relationship (perhaps this is why homosexual "marriages" tend to be especially short-lived); that sex and love are are not identical feelings and should not be confused with each other (though a combination of the two probably pleases people more often and more deeply than their attempted enjoyment separately).

These are some of the guides to behavior which the parent, if he believes in them, can try to transmit to his child. The child can accept them or not—and will usually exercise his prerogative without informing his parent of his choices. But even if he rejects the parent's views for the moment—or the year—he may return to them in a year or more, or be influenced by them in some way. The parent should not judge his success by his *immediate* effect.

Most of what we would call sexual skill is not, however, information, principle, or even technique. It consists of the ability to make and maintain close relationships with peer members of the opposite sex, from which some sexual relationships will normally, almost inevitably, develop. They will develop, that is, if the youth does not have special psychological or (very rarely) physical problems that produce impotence, frigidity, fear, or guilt. In such cases, professional therapy may be required, or special instruction in sexual techniques. To us, however, sexual competence does *not* mean skill with sexual technique. Whatever benefits are offered by the manuals, picture books, and movies on sexual techniques derive, we believe, from these two simple principles discussed elsewhere in connection with other areas of human behavior: that sexual behavior (as with any other area of achievement) should produce pleasure, satisfaction, reward in its own right, because it is a normal need that one profits generally from fulfilling; and that a flexible problem-solving attitude is the surest way of finding satisfaction in sex (or any other area of behavior) when difficulties develop.

Sibling Problems

To the extent that the child's problems with his brothers and sisters are similar to those he has with others socially, they have already been discussed. There are also differences, however, and in any case the parent has more direct control over how her child handles his companions within the home than those outside.

A major and potentially useful distinction of the child's relations with his siblings is that they are inevitable. He cannot withdraw from them. They face him when he gets up in the morning and when he goes to bed at night. He shares with them his parents, meals, relatives, trips, sicknesses, household duties, pets. He must develop some kind of relationship with them even if he dislikes them and would not voluntarily choose them as friends.

The parent may say, and repeat to her deathbed, "You must always love each other." While this is an ideal state of affairs within a family—or, indeed, among any people anywhere—it seems to be relatively seldom achieved, at least not stably for long periods of time, particularly when the children are still living together, since proximity does aggravate conflict.

What this means is that whatever social problems the child has are likely to show in exaggerated form in the home, and very special ones will appear besides, which involve unique conditions of inescapable closeness, treatment as a part of a group with brothers and sisters, competition for parental attention, special attention by the parent, and shared family activities.

What is uniquely important about the child's behavior in the family is probably his relationship to his parents rather than to his siblings, and perhaps also the ways of behaving toward children that he learns from his parents and may apply to *his* children. If ever the pattern of relationship between parents and children is going to be improved, the change will probably best be initiated by parents who set out with their newborn babies and proceed through the years deliberately to break the pattern of how their parents treated them and to institute improved ways with their children.

The parent does have special power in the family situation to observe and correct the child's behavior with other children, namely his siblings—far more than he has the power to affect social behavior outside the home. He should use this influence, keeping in mind its broader implications for behavior outside the home. For example, a child should not be excused and protected when teasing his brothers and sisters, merely because he looks angelic or acts courteously to the parent. His teasing will *not* be protected outside the home. Nor should the parent try to break up a fight by demanding that brothers and sisters love each other. This is a desirable goal for all human beings, but it is not an effective way to break up a fight, since the words are meaningless in the situation, and it has no value as a method out of the home.

Styles of problem-solving in the family get set and generalized for later life. Some common sibling problems include *jealousy* and *sharing*. Jealousy should be treated as objectively as possible by parents, maintaining a vigorous standard of fairness for the jealousy to break against. Sharing requires that rules be set about ownership of property, explicit conditions of sharing, sharing as trading-off toys, and other specific situations, without platitudes about being "good" or "unselfish."

There are many ways of training children. Parents cannot and need not agree on all of them, nor can all parents agree on the same goals for children. Originality and heterogeneity should be not only allowed but encouraged.

Too often, however, parents get bound up in pseudo-goals and in conflicting means for reaching these goals. They need clear guidelines on which to operate, as with *tattling* and *responsibility sharing.* In connection with tattling, parents must know that children like to get one another into trouble, and therefore not take "tales" literally without considering the *use* the child may be making of them. Responsibility sharing is both necessary and feasible; children can share chores and learn to take turns with privileges as well as duties. Many adults feel that when they were children a sibling got the best "deal" or "got the dirty end of the stick" at home because equity and sharing were not followed well.

The home, then, is as crucial a place for learning social living as the child's life with friends and groups outside the home. But it is at home that the parent has her best chance to exercise control and influence, and it is there that her chief efforts should be directed toward social objectives.

CHAPTER X

Developing Skills and Talents

ALONG WITH LEARNING the fundamentals of social survival, the development of talents and skills is the most important part of general education. If a child has some special talent or talents, such as art, music, mechanical inventiveness—and most children, if carefully considered, would probably be found to have one or more—the cultivation of these attributes may become the focal point of his or her education. Thus, special talents—those ways in which a given child is exceptional—may provide vocational and educational objectives of a highly important nature. They also point to the ways in which children as children, and after becoming adults, can derive special satisfactions outside of their regular education or employment.

Talents are not limited to the arts (music, drawing, sculpturing, and the like) but may also include athletic prowess (for example, ability to run fast, jump high, or combine talents to make an all-around good athlete), combinations of talents such as found in engineering or architecture (such as spatial relations, art, math, and abstract comprehension abilities), craftsmanship—say, in working with wood, in gardening, or on automobiles—and so on almost interminably. In fact, one could not exhaustively list all talents, because whatever is prized by the society or special groups in society, or even valued by an individual, could be considered a talent (cooking, crocheting, mounting rocks, climbing mountains, to name a few examples). Ability to debate well, acting effectively, dancing agilely, putting people at ease socially are further examples of talents of great value variously to individuals and to society generally.

Skills, on the other hand, important as they are, may be considered less unusual, and qualitatively less refined or exceptional in the general population. We all develop some skill in walking, running, talking, even usually dancing and swimming. We tend to think of these skills as basic to being human, social living, or survival, as necessary for daily living and communication. Our concern in this chapter is to discuss both talents and skills generally, and how to evaluate and develop them in the child.

It is very difficult to judge the extent of talents in children. There are few, if any, *objective* ways to measure talent. One must depend mostly on the opinions of experts in the field involved. If you wished to know whether your ten-year-old's talent for, say, playing the piano was exceptional, obtaining the opinion of respected piano teachers would be the best way to get answers to your query.

Talents are also often judged by the way a child performs in a contest or recital. Winning at musical talent shows, concerts, or recitals before professional judges, is often the sign that can start an exceptional person on a career in music. Similarly, one may enter drawings, paintings, models, handicraft, and other works in contests whose purpose is to recognize and encourage unusual talent. It does not follow, however, that if one's child does not win or place in such a contest that he or she is not talented. If a dozen gifted children enter an art or musical contest, by definition very few win or place, and a child down the list might, in the long run, turn out to be the most talented of the lot. Those who win are most likely talented—if all judgments are set up to be as fair and valid as possible—but those who do not win can seek other ways of reinforcement such as the opinions of knowledgeable relatives, personal contacts with experts, and opinions of informed peers.

The flowering of talent, like any kind of achievement, depends upon hard work and disciplined application to one's goals if it is to be developed to anywhere near its full potential. The talent is not a residue of ability, waiting to be tapped like water in a pipe, but is, rather, a complex assortment of capability, work and study skills, social encouragement, opportunity, and perseverance. That "Talent will out" is chancy belief. True, the talented person may have less trouble acquiring high-level skills in music, art, or mechanics, compared to the average person; but the talent per se is no single vein, no entity that can be called to an appearance fullblown. It is not even observable in some instances, without cultivation. The world is probably full of bright and gifted persons who never developed their potentialities even to a point where talent is noticeable. How naive and wasteful it is to think that singing talent will "develop itself," or that one can rise to high levels without hard work! Athletes train relentlessly, no matter how great their physical equipment, they never act as if their capabilities as sprinters, hurdlers, or high-jumpers "will out" and all they have to do is get on the playing field and display their talents for all to see.

One common error that parents make is to rely on what they think the child's talents are as the primary element in motivating them to develop the talent. "You know, Sammy is so gifted as a singer, but he doesn't work at it," a parent laments. The parent often relies on repeated expressions of the presence of the talent, implying to the child that the talent itself should be a ticket to recognition, success, or acclaim, when the emphasis should be placed on the *development* of the talent. When you keep telling a child that he is good just because of gifts he was born with, you do not motivate him for achievement. By such an approach you tend, as a parent, to make the talent, rather than achievement (the development of the talent), the important issue.

Handling talent that is flourishing is also a problem. Sometimes gifted children may be handled very narrowly by their parents or teachers. Sending a child to a special music or art school may be good in many cases, but it should not lead to a narrowing of the child's development away from the ordinary, daily matters of education, training, self-discipline, and self-control. The talent is not sufficient, important as it may be. Regard for social development—such as ordinary play with peers—should not be disregarded in the case of the talented child, no matter how gifted he may be.

Besides emphasizing as we have above that talents should be judged carefully, and should not be permitted to exercise total dominance in the child's development, it is important to suggest that talents involve a responsibility. From the view of society, people who have unusual talent can be held to *owe* the development of it to themselves and to society. This does not mean that the individual should not enjoy his talent, or developing it or sharing it with others, but it does mean that, in a well structured society, he should be encouraged to develop as fruitfully as he can—and be trained in a sense of responsibility about it. It is, likewise, a responsibility of society to ferret out the talented ones and aid their development. It is a joint task of the individual child and those responsible for him to develop his talent, and the task of society to make fruition as likely as possible. The same principles should apply, of course, to the more modest talents (or skills) characterizing most children—there should be the same joint responsibility to develop whatever skills can be brought to social usefulness. No one should be ignored regarding such responsibility, however meager or inconspicuous his talents and skills.

Skills may be very modest, but in the personal economy of the individual child such ability is as important as the large talent. The average child has to develop his skills in playing, in modest art or musical or athletic accomplishment, in hunting, fishing, or games with a sense of worth that develops society's welfare. This is what holds him (and the rest of us) together psychologically.

Social, Language, and Other Practical Arts

We have cited the relevance of handicrafts, athletic prowess, the arts, as skills. There are also many social skills which all of us need to survive and flourish, and which the child should be introduced to as early as is practicable. There are communication skills such as speaking to others (to obtain what you want), replying courteously when spoken to (to maintain good will), taking responsibility to carry on a conversation (to establish rapport). Even very young children, when visited by a neighboring child, begin to develop some of these skills—helping the visiting child to toys, letting him look at one's books, offering him a drink or a sweet. Parents can help the host child develop these skills by making such leading remarks as, "Billy, you may take Ralph to the play area in the rec room if you like" or "If you want to show Ralph your new bike, Billy, I'll have some hot chocolate for you when you come in later." These cues give the child a chance to follow a lead set by parental example on how to be friendly and a good host to a visitor.

Or the parent may instruct a child on yielding a seat on the bus to an old person or helping another person retrieve a lost or dropped article, and so on. Social and communication skills can be considered the art of making the other person comfortable, administering to him in some minor but appreciated ways, or obtaining what you want or need from him. Simply to ignore others or their needs on the grounds that they mean nothing to you is to ignore the base for establishing and maintaining mutually advantageous relationships.

Parents often pass by opportunities to instruct the child in social amenities, feeling that there is plenty of time later to do this. However, as with language development, reading, and athletic skills, the earlier the parent starts with the child, and the more consistently he instructs the child, the easier it is for the child to develop social maturity. Not all social maturity is dependent upon grace in social behavior, of course, but such skill helps noticeably in this regard.

Sharing and taking turns are two very important nuclei around which the parent can help the child develop these skills. Children begin as naturally selfish. The baby grabs, as does the young child—partly as exploration, partly as matter of immediate possessiveness. But the older child, after about four or five, should learn to yield to the social amenities to a considerable extent. He learns this in nursery school and kindergarten, in the context of sharing with others, which makes these schooling experiences very valuable to all children.

At the table, sharing and taking turns can be taught. Each child at the table can pass something; each child can offer a dish or an item of the menu (bread, butter, or the like) to another before he serves himself. Parents can center easily on this kind of simple social skill and make considerable headway in a short time. The taking turns can come from such behavior as clearing the table, setting the table, or serving hot dishes from the stove. Dishwashing and many domestic skills are often unpopular with children and adolescents, but some chores along these lines are a part of family living in most households, and are the bases for the first extensive training in serving others.

The handling of TV watching, record playing, and musical instrument playing can also figure in the development of social skills, especially in the home. Some children station themselves before the TV set upon arriving at home and stay there, without regard to other matters, until pulled away by force, by hunger, or by pulling the electrical cord. Parents can increase social skills as well as general discipline and training by making TV watching *contingent* upon other matters having been attended to—clothes changed afer school, room picked up, animals fed, table for evening meal set, yard mowed, or snow cleared. All of these matters are part of running a household; the child should do his share. His share can be enhanced if he gets what he wants (TV watching, for example) *after* he has played his role in relation to others. Playing the piano or practicing a sport can obstruct other gainful activities, especially if the child is good at it, and the parent may give priority to such activity because it educates or pleases the child. Such activities are important, but they should not screen out the common necessities of daily living together, general education, or ordinary social amenities. The practicing is fine, but it should not be permitted to take the place of broad-based social behavior, and it need not do so if the parent balances the give-and-take he or she can control directly with the child.

The parental role here is one of structuring the situations so that there is optimal opportunity for the child to behave and learn what is desirable, and at the same time minimize the distracted or nonproductive behavior.

An example of parental structuring is shown in the following case:

> *Bennie liked to read the "funny papers" each morning, and especially on Sundays. These papers could take up an hour or more of her time, to the detriment of getting her to the breakfast table, her animals fed, her room cleaned up, preparation for*

school accomplished, and the like. Hours of threats and cajolery did nothing to manage the situation. Finally, the mother hit on the very obvious plan of simply putting aside the papers before Bennie arose and dressed, and then giving them to her upon the performance of her chores.

Each parent can think of many similar situations. What he or she needs to do in these cases is to find the natural leverage that is open to parental control—in this case taking away the "funny papers" and then eliciting from the child the behavior required by practical necessities before the child got to his "goodies." The "goodies" are fine—there is nothing wrong with reading the "funnies"; in fact it helps the parent in training the child to have available such rewards that the child appreciates. They just have to follow (as reinforcements) the other activities the parents require and the household economy demands. This is effective structuring; this is using what the child wants as a reinforcer; this is getting the child through the activities required in effective family living.

Vocational and Employment Skills

The child begins to learn early that he is expected to take his place in the world of work someday. He speculates about it; he is queried about it throughout his developing years. Skill development, in the sense of work and study habits—academic and achievement skills, as dealt with in Chapter XI—is vitally important to the child's successful employment as an adult, and should be started early.

Many parents think that work is oppressive, or at least to be avoided if possible. They display their own lack of enthusiasm for their "calling." But the child who learns to like and profit from work and from study is likely to make a more productive person as an adult, and more likely to infuse others with enthusiasm and respect for his work—most importantly in the case of his own children. A good basis for training in this area of life is to start early with small chores and household responsibilities.

Each of us has to learn to do a lot of things he would like to avoid, and to tolerate and accept some tasks he dislikes. The "spoiled" adult is one who cannot get past the things he likes to do to the things he has to do in order to maintain economic solvency or necessary social communication. The adult who has deteriorated in—or perhaps never gained—social, vocational, or employment skills tends (further) to drift, or to decline in his resourcefulness and to narrow his opportunities.

Students can be brought to see the "pay-off" for attending responsibly to their lessons, and adults can be brought to see the value in sustained application, for their goals are elusive or visionary or marginal unless they have the stamina and perseverance to pursue them.

Parents often say that their chosen work is not what they would do if they had their lives to live over again. Somewhere in the vicinity of 40 to 50 percent of the adult population report, upon questioning, that they wish another occupation had been chosen. This is true partly because all of us can envision a "perfect" world for ourselves where work and play would exist in some vastly different proportion for us. Adult dissatisfactions are also a reflection of the poor training they have likely had for decision-making and problem-solving in the areas of work, study and self-application generally. We tend to infect our children with these loose, poorly conceived attitudes without meaning to do so; our example here is more vivid and enduring than the empty words we may say about doing one's work well and enjoying life to the fullest.

The Self-Concept and Self-Respect

Self-respect and one's concept of oneself are popular topics in psychology today. As we have indicated in many other parts of this book, a person's estimate of himself and his self-respect are born not out of some psychic mist, but specifically and faithfully out of the way he does what he is supposed to do. People generally have a good self-concept if they are able to measure up to their aspirations and intentions (goals), with performance.

On the other hand, when there is great discrepancy between what one intends or aspires to and what he actually achieves, the hiatus between the two sets of conditions produces stress and a poor self-concept.

Teaching a child to value his labors and to set viable goals he can achieve (and be reinforced for) is a valuable service to him in preparation for his adult life. He cannot find self-respect or build self-confidence in the psychologist's office (even though it may prepare the way), or by using tranquilizing drugs—at least not for long. The stuff of life that gives us our self-respect consists of our handiwork, our achievement, what satisfaction our behavior earns us; and our behavior is built of many small actions we take hour by hour, day by day, and year by year. These are the building blocks that make up one's self-esteem, self-concept, self-confidence, self-assurance—the *self* in all its perspectives.

Society's Role in Developing Talents

Does society take responsibility for ferreting out and developing talents? Yes and no. Contests, recitals, rewards, and scholarships are common to encourage and develop talents among children and youth. Much more could be done, however.

Over the last four or five decades, an increasing number of children have completed high school—a rise from about 30 percent graduated from high school in the 1920's (from among all who entered grade school) to about 70 percent (or better) graduated from high school today. This is an encouraging trend, to be sure; but many children have been neglected in the past, and many skills have gone undeveloped and many talents ignored; and many adults present problems today because of this fact. Today we are doing better, but we still have a long way to go.

There are hundreds of millions of people over the world who do not know how to read or write at even the third grade (American equivalent) level. At the college level, dropouts may be as high as 50 to 75 percent at the close of the freshman year, although some of those who drop out finish later (as do some high school students who drop out before their regular graduation time). Much skill and talent—from the ordinary to the extraordinary—is not being recognized or developed in the United States. And statistics are even less encouraging in most other parts of the world!

The "culturally disadvantaged" are being much discussed today. Great segments of the population are underfed, poorly educated, and badly housed, and receive little cultural encouragement. Hundreds of thousands of children never have their talents recognized or are never offered opportunity to develop them, and, of course, there are many thousands among them who have extraordinary potentialities but die totally unrecognized or wasted.

Pertinent here is the condition of schools and the relatively poor curriculum found in them in the disadvantaged community compared to schools in many non-disadvantaged areas. One high school in an "advantaged" community offered six times as many courses in foreign languages, two or three times as many in the sciences, three times as many vocational and business courses, as well as some unique courses in art, psychology, and sociology, compared to a nearby high school in the same city but in an economically poor area. Even ordinary skills cannot be developed in the disadvantaged community, let alone the higher-level talents that should be recognized and cultivated. In fact, special school and community efforts are needed for this purpose far more in the poor areas than in the other areas, because parents and other social forces are less likely to perform this function.

We have, then, two broad classes of children who are not getting the opportunities needed to develop skills and talents: those whom we might call the "dropouts," many of whom are from "advantaged" backgrounds; and the "left outs," who do not even enter good educational and related systems. We might add a third "loss" group, the socially-emotionally-physically handicapped, who seldom get started very well in the first place, whose skills and talents have not been recognized, and who have been shunted away into culturally barren institutions and mostly forgotten.

CHAPTER XI

Achieving in School

FROM THE TIME the child starts school—nursery school, kindergarten, or the conventional first grade—until he completes his formal education or training, his school life is a vitally formative experience. Complain as we may about the quality of formal education, school experiences have far-reaching effect in the child's life, and often set the stage for later successes or failures.

It is fashionable in some groups to play down the desirability of achievement in school. Some say it should be mostly "fun," and thereby seem to contrast schoolwork with pleasure, thinking that one cannot get much fun out of achieving in school. Others, like us, disagree, believing that achieving in school can be both work and pleasure. We see no purpose in splitting these two concerns, or in artificially pitting them against each other. The greatest human satisfaction probably lies in a combination of the two.

Achievement in the broad sense does not depend upon school experiences, although the latter may enhance and provide opportunities for achievement. Many inventors, artists, writers, and people with agrarian or manual skills and talents, among others, have done their good work without benefit of formal school training. In fact, some have succeeded in spite of bad achievement reports from school.

What, then, is achievement, what is its importance at school, and how may it be best accomplished?

Simply stated, achievement is first of all the accumulation of knowledge or skill. We say a child has achieved well when he has learned what he had to know to pass a Boy Scout merit badge requirement—collecting bug specimens or coins and telling about them, learning lifesaving in the water, or whatever. It means the child can now *perform* (or has shown this performance in the past, and can call upon it now) in some way he was not able to perform before.

In this sense, achievement is a skill level or skill base upon which more achievement can be built. If a child has learned how to swim up to 50 feet in a summer program, this is no small matter in itself; but it is also the basis for extending his swimming prowess to hundreds of feet, and for learning complex variations, such as lifesaving and racing.

Achievement in this sense is often never lost. It may deteriorate with disuse, but usually the achievement base never wholly passes. Even if it is largely forgotten, the skill base (as in swimming, skating, singing) can, barring neurological complications, be reactivated and brought up to its original level in a shorter time that it took to acquire the achievement in the first place. The achievement base may often become dormant, or diminished, but is seldom obliterated.

We rely on achievement in ourselves and others. We believe the dentist "knows how" to put in a filling or pull a tooth. He has *achieved* this skill status by virtue of his training and experience. He has *achieved* a skill—and he *uses* this skill. Likewise the lawyer has achieved his knowledge of and skill in practicing law—he knows what to do. And so on, to hundreds of possible examples of our dependency on the achievement of others.

Achievement is observable. We note this when we comment that a person has made a million dollars. It is visible in some way—or could be made visible if the owner desired. When we call upon skills like those the dentist or lawyer possesses, we then *require the achievement to be shown*. Achievement can be put on display under specifiable conditions.

A second characteristic of achievement is that it is usually a complex set of skills woven together to meet some common human need. The skills of a lawyer or a dentist are an amalgamation of many areas of achievement, such as reading, manual dexterity, verbal expression, written expression, thinking, and problem-solving. The person who has made a lot of money has, likewise, woven into one fabric, so to speak, many skills, and the outcome—for better or worse—is that he has accumulated (achieved) much money, or goods standing for money.

Often children, and sometimes parents, think that achievement of a high order is due to some kind of luck or happenstance. The child or his parent who would like the child to achieve well in athletics—say high-jumping—may think that one just goes out jumping a few poles and has thereby achieved skill if he has any talent at the task. Running, balancing, timing, muscle development, learning how to fall correctly, and other subskills all figure in achieving at high jumping. It is a complex set of motor and other skills woven into a standard outcome—jumping.

We do not usually gain achievement, then, without giving considerable attention to parts that make up the achievement effort.

Achievement also builds personal satisfaction and confidence. It is by the fruits of our efforts that we judge ourselves, and are judged by others. A person who achieves well—say a child in school—is generally given some credit, some reinforcement, by his peers, his teachers, and his parents.

Conversely, if one tries and does not succeed, he is at least somewhat affected in a negative way. He wonders why; what went wrong; how he can improve the next time. The lack of achievement brings problems, loss of confidence, and often personal and emotional difficulties.

Think of how glad the young toddler is when he drops a ball and it bounces back to him, how excited the preschooler is when he makes a toy "work," how pleased the kindergarten child is when he knows the answer to some question or can show that he is beginning to read. These are all worthwhile achievements: they build confidence; they earn reinforcement; they pave the way for more achievement.

If achievement is important in all these respects—representing knowledge, amalgamation of skills, and the source of confidence and self-esteem—why is it not more sought after and gained?

Actually, most of us are achieving most of the time, whether we know it or not, whether we intend to or not. As long as we are alive and interacting with our environments, we are usually achieving. Men who have worked a lifetime in fields or factories may learn late in life how to play cards, or paint, or build with wood; women who have been in offices all their lives may in their fifties or sixties learn new ways to cook, crochet, or do politicking. One never stops learning—and achieving—though the process may not always be voluntary. A man may have to learn new skills when he loses his job, or a woman when she is divorced and has no income. Or when one marries a foreigner.

Helping the child to understand that achievement does not depend upon formal schooling is important. Having him learn that he will, one way or another, lead a life of achievement is also important. One should try to develop the attitude among children that achievement—like breathing—is part of life and will go on and on.

Achievement, then, should not be associated just with formal schooling, such as learning the spelling lesson (important as it is), but includes activities of the entire day in and out of school.

Suppose, though, that the parent wants to upgrade achievement considerations in her child. Suppose she wants to optimize this facet of life. What can the parent do to set a style *for* achievement? There are many actions she can take. Among them are these:

1.   The parent can develop the habit of openly admiring achievement in others. She can remark to the child what "old Mrs. Jones" has achieved even though she is confined to crutches. She can comment on what the community, or the local school, or some other group has achieved in some visible way (raising money for a worthy cause, getting a dangerous bridge fixed, building a park for children to play in). This sets a style.

2.   The parent can reinforce (show interest in, encourage, reward) the child's own achievement record—tests passed well at school, yes, but much more: good attendance at school meetings, having kept his room in reasonable order for a week, a "good turn" done his neighbor such as bringing in his newspaper when he was out of town, helping a child in trouble.

3.   She can base achievement rewards first on what the child naturally likes to do. Begin where the child already is; use his inclinations (watch his behavior) and reward his achievement in these areas. This does not need to be a conspicuous talent, such as playing the piano at age five; but, more simply, clear speech, the expression of a wise attitude toward a peer, the sharing of toys with a friend, coming to the parent with problems the child could not handle on his own. All of these can be reinforced (rewarded, otherwise encouraged).

4. She can help the child to recognize and reward the achievement of others—his sister's apron made at school, although perhaps clumsily tailored; his mother's good cherry pie; his teacher's way of explaining something; a friend's playing music he likes to hear; his father's reading the stories he likes to have read to him; and any other achievement he can learn to see and appreciate in others.

5. She can direct present skills to pivot the way to other skills, as encouraged in previous chapters. The child likes TV, well and good. He gets to see it, contingent *upon his arithmetic's being completed. This is a kind of double reinforcement, or double encouragement: encouraging his preferences, but also upgrading needed achievement (in weak or reluctant areas) by hooking them to areas of behavior or achievement in which he is already strong. He learns to respect the already-achieved behavior and the behavior he still has to grapple with. This is self-discipline in growth!*

No one of these procedures for encouraging achievement will necessarily work wonders, but they are *likely* to reward your efforts to establish an achievement base with your child—and this is vitally important for his future.

Specific Application to School and Classroom

Achievement in school must be a realistic objective of formal education. If a child has not achieved in school, then his time and the time of everyone concerned is likely to have been wasted. What he *may* have gained to apply in his life outside of school can only be guessed at, and is often a weak excuse for failure to set and achieve reasonable and valuable goals in the school. School achievement is a primary concern of the child (and his family) for the many years of his formal education. How can the parent use the present school conditions the most for her child?

> *First, the parent should get to know the teacher, the school curriculum, and the general character-istics of the school and classroom in which her child (or children) attend school.*

Practically all parents know about PTA meetings to get acquainted with the child's teacher and school setting, but not all make use of them. All parents should attend parent meetings at school. If they cannot attend such regular meetings, there is always the possibility of other meetings with the teacher or principal privately. These should be utilized at least a time or two each year for the child. If the meetings are poorly organized or used by the school, the parent and the PTA should demand better conditions.

> *Second, the parent should get copies of the teacher's curriculum plans for each course (such as arithmetic, reading, or history) so that she knows as many details as possible about what her child will be confronted with in his daily classes. The teacher's curriculum plans may include copies of the child's textbooks, a reading list for outside-of-class reading and reporting, or a lab manual. Sometimes the school will not allow the parent to have a copy of a textbook. While we do not think this is a good practice on the school's part, the parent can still obtain other textbooks similar in nature to the one the child is using. What one seeks here is systematic exposure to a given content area, such as arithmetic or science, which the child is to learn about, so that the parent can know and support what her child is supposed to be learning.*

It is too costly for some parents to build a library of their own at home for a child (or several children), so such a desirable practice must be limited. Used books can often be obtained economically. Workbooks, placed at various age and grade levels for all common subjects, can also be obtained. The parent can weave in the child's work in these supplemental textbooks or workbooks to fit his regular homework or home study programs from school when achievement is faltering. This is not to suggest that more work be piled on the child, but that the parent consider additional sources of help for the child when they might make his work easier.

The teacher's report cards each six or nine weeks are not enough to tell you, the parent, all you should know about your child's achievements. This brings us to the next point in aiding your child's achievement at school:

> *Third, get a blank copy of the report card to see what achievement and conduct items are registered on the card. Know how often the report card is made up, and when; and whether individual interviews or conferences are offered the parent (especially in the first three grades) in lieu of or to supplement a formal report card.*

Upon gaining knowledge of the reporting system, you are able to judge your child's achievement somewhat more broadly than just by reading the teacher's comments (important as these are). Add to this information your own observations of the child's work in arithmetic, or science, or reading, so that you have a much broader base for understanding your child's achievement, his strengths and weaknesses. You may, in time, want to move the child to another school, or have to move him to another school because of changes in family plans, and the above-cited types of information will give you a reasonable basis for making decisions about such moves. It is best to have your data on your child's achievement updated each semester, or at least each year, so that you are not confronted all at once with some glaring deficiency in his work, or some other educational problem you should have known about but did not.

> *Fourth, get to know your child's reactions to his school, his teacher, and other aspects of his daily living at school. Parents often dismiss the child's attitudes about school and teachers as mere childish opinions, or they may hold the child's opinions in too high (biased) regard, and in either case fail to build an objective base for their own parental decisions.*

In many cases, where the parents have ultimately needed to transfer the child to a different school (public or private), the transfer decision came only after neglect of the child's plight at school, not listening carefully and often to his opinions, and not taking his feelings properly into consideration before (and during or after) the transfer. Parents often act as if "getting it over with" were the main consideration, hoping that a transfer of the child to a different school will solve all the problems and that they (the parents) can slip back into complacency again. Parents can *never* leave the whole matter of schooling to the school, without being faced with surprises, disappointments, and crises!

> *A fifth point concerns how to increase self-discipline and self-control in the child. This point refers to having a fairly clear (but flexible) daily schedule for the child to follow. As previous discussions have indicated, this will cover getting-up and going-to-bed times and work, study, and play times, the little chores and household obligations the child is assigned about the house, and other details such as music practice and lessons, swimming practice, recreational activities.*

The importance of this overall structure or scheduling of time cannot be overemphasized. Not that every minute has to be accounted for, or that change and flexibility are precluded. Some parents do overschedule their children, but it is not this excessive type of control that is referred to here. It is better to have some structure that is reliable than to drift, then suddenly wake up to the fact that you, the parent, and everyone else concerned has wasted a lot of money, time, or effort (such as paying for music lessons without any accomplishment visible) and are disgusted with the whole ineffectual situation. Better to use foresight and planning so that when changes are called for (as they usually are), they can be made intelligently and economically with regard to the child's efforts as well as to your parental efforts!

> *Sixth, set the child's requirements (study, chores, curfews) in the context of the rewards or reinforcements he wishes to gain. This has been the theme of this whole book—to set contingencies so that what you want gets accomplished as part of the arrangement whereby the child, too, gets what he wants. Such a system is pivotal for the desired, long-lasting results.*

No one of us gets what he wants without some strings attached, or paying some price. All we do, or get, or earn, or have as pleasure comes with a kind of price tag on it: we have to earn the money, arrange for the time, set up the conditions, engage the help or advice of others, plan and work for some specific goals—all life is contingent upon some effort before the payoff. You are doing your child an immense service if you make this conditional nature of his behavior clear, reliable, and fair!

> *Seventh, keep up your interest in and firmness with your child's accomplishments by clearly*

noticing his efforts and accomplishments from time to time. Let a grandmother know in a letter how well Johnny is playing his guitar, or how hard Susan is working at her sewing. Let there be periodic public notice of the child's efforts. These come as a kind of "bonus" and can be very reassuring and reinforcing to the child, as well as to the parent.

This latter point can be considered part of the sixth point—about reinforcing (rewarding) efforts—but is really an extension of the latter, a thinking-out over time of reinforcing efforts. One should not be anxious about rewarding the child. It should be developed as a natural part of the parent's behavior, and flow freely at as many opportunities as possible. This kind of reward-flow helps the child to develop self-control and self-discipline without making him dependent upon your every word. He knows at the end of the summer he has done well in his athletic work, his yard-mowing, his music lessons. Something like your letter to grandmother citing this achievement is a kind of capstone to the whole effort.

The eighth point, implied in much of the above discussion, is that of having recourse to talking over the child's situation (whether good or not) with teacher or principal. The parent can gain from visiting the school sometimes just to say "hello" and to maintain good communication with the school, whether there is a problem at hand or not. To show up at school only when a problem exists narrows your base of operation and tends to reinforce, unwittingly, the desirability of problems occuring, if only then do you show interest in the school.

This is perhaps the commonest mistake the vast majority of parents make: showing up at, or communicating with, the school only in a crisis or near-crisis. This gives a flavor to parent-school relations that may be nonconstructive because of sensitivity to conflict and misunderstanding and not well calculated to help the overall progress of the child. Too often, in such cases, feelings run high and the issue of the child's welfare is lost in the battle between parent and school as to who is "right," who is "to blame," and who should do what to correct matters.

It should always be kept in mind that the purpose of the child's school experiences and achievement are to bring his humanness into fruition, and any measures that do not contribute to this goal should not distract either parent or school. There is a combined project here of inestimable value to the child and to society. All measures should enhance it!

PART III

HANDLING COMMON PROBLEMS

CHAPTER XII

Sources and Viewpoints

THE PREVIOUS SECTIONS of this book have dealt with the goals, methods, and techniques of training children in self-discipline and achievement. Finally we come to the handling of specific problems, a point at which many books for parents begin—and end.

Many parents, after all, are interested only in advice about this or that practical problem. Some readers may have grown impatient with our first two sections; some may skip to this part. "What we want to know," they might say, "is how to get our child over bed-wetting, or not studying or staying out late, or being disobedient or disrespectful, or hating us. We need practical advice, not theory or principles."

To them we would repeat here: if you are forever going to try to solve practical problems on a day-to-day improvised basis, you will not profit as much as you could from science, from the experience of others, or from your own experience. Nor will you, as effectively as you could, *prevent* problems from arising. Nor will you know what to do in the constantly arising *new* situations, from what you could have learned ahead of time.

It is far better to deal with problems on a day-to-day improvised basis than not to deal with them at all—or to apply certain principles you have heard and stick to them stubbornly even when they do not solve the problems that confront you. For example, you may think that you should never speak or act in anger with your child—so you never act at all when your son swears at you, because you are angry. It may be better to act calmly and with a plan to control the swearing, but it is almost certainly better to act in anger (provided it is not extreme or physically damaging) than not to act at all and let the swearing continue—and continually enrage you.

Our plea throughout this book, however, is for well-considered behavior on your part—well-considered in the sense that it takes advantage of all the information and experience and thought you can assemble *to produce as effective a result as possible.* Thus whether you act in anger or from a particular principle or theory to try to change your child's swearing, it should with the paramount consideration of whether it is likely to change the problem behavior, without creating more problems or having adverse effects that outweigh the gain. In other words, the problem should be solved with overall gain in the total behavior of the child.

We have tried, therefore, to prepare the ground for this section by presenting goals, methods, and techniques founded upon research and experience that provide *systematic* guidance about how to go about solving problems in training your children. They should also provide attitudes and principles that give practical guidance in how to handle concrete situations.

The Preventive Concept

Even more important, such an approach—of planning to handle the training of children even before problems arise, in ways best calcuated to reach predetermined goals—gives hope of preventing or avoiding problems. You need not wait for problems to arise. You plan, really, to train the child so that goals can be achieved, rather than waiting for problems to arise.

Suppose, for example, you want your child to do his school work as well as his learning ability permits (not his "motivation," mind you, since that may depend upon how well he has learned to handle his work!). Do you have to wait for poor grades or bad study habits or a teacher's report of his "laziness" to show up? By no means! (How many parents, however, *do* take preventive action?) You *can* train your child from the day he begins school to treat his assignments with care and respect, to let you know what is required of him and to show you his work, to know that mistakes and incompetence are necessary steps on the route to skill and achievement, to do his highest priority work first before taking on secondary work or recreation.

You would thus be doing positive preventive training that would help to stop problems from arising. If, nevertheless, poor grades or bad study habits should develop, you would have to change your method (though not the *concept* of training). You would yourself have a chance to profit from having failed to some extent and could analyze how—but it would be a failure of a particular effort, rather than neglect, and you would have a better chance to find a successful method than if you never tried at all.

Advantages of the Systematic Approach

Furthermore, you gain from using a *systematic* approach. You gain because you need not treat every problem as if it were unique. You have attitudes, principles, and techniques available to you that can be applied to almost any situation that might arise.

The approach used with the problem of studying

mentioned above, for example, can just as well be applied to a problem of work around the house, to acquiring skill in playing baseball, or to learning how to drive a car—even, in large part, to how to date a girl.

With such generally applicable methods you can find a comfort and confidence in your power to solve problems that improvisation can seldom provide. A world of constant surprises, where each new problem your child displays disrupts your life before you have ways of coping with it, will keep you off balance and inefficient in managing your own life as well as in training your children.

You can be properly humble about your ability to cope with constantly changing problems and at the same time be relatively stable and serene in the knowledge that you have tools that can be used, with a reasonable chance for success. And that, in addition, you know how to go about modifying these tools as necessary to adapt to changing circumstances, and to measure their effectiveness and continue to adapt them to be successful.

Newspaper and magazine columnists on personal problems have always been popular in this country for the practicality of their advice, often combined with wit and simplicity of writing. Much of what they advise seems to be about as good in the specific situations described to them as professional counselors could devise within the severe limits of time and space that the column permits.

Two major ingredients that are integral parts of the best kind of professional advice and that the columnists lack, on the other hand, are the *systematic* approach and *followup*, combined perhaps with somewhat less confidence, brashness, or positiveness on the part of the professional.

The popular columnist usually improvises according to the situation presented, with little regard for principles of learning or training. What consistency he displays is more likely to be of mood or general attitude than of a systematic view of what the most effective training methods are. He may *always* take the view of "spare the rod and spoil the child," or of giving the child his head, or of having the parent express his feelings, or of communicating honestly—but the *relationship* of the method to effective learning is seldom given primary and systematic attention.

The columnist does offer the reader the advantage of specific advice, of a concrete action that can be taken immediately. This is of more direct help than what the nondirective or psychoanalytic professional usually provides. But we hope to add to the common-sense kind of advice or suggestions the advantages accruing from a systematic approach, so that each new problem need not be treated as if it were unique and required an entirely distinctive approach.

We hope that by presenting *some* solutions to *some* common problems we can make it possible for you to apply the systematic approaches and methods illustrated to new problems that will arise. You will, in other words, have learned how to go about solving problems, rather than learning the solutions to all problems that can arise (which is impossible).

Followup

Furthermore, there is almost never followup, modification, adaptation, or radical change in what the columnist recommends. He recommends, in a paragraph or two, and that is the end of the matter. If the advice makes sense to many people, or is witty, it is popular. Whether it solves the problem, or whether the problem stays solved for very long, or whether it is an efficient solution, or whether it will need to be modified, are considerations that hardly ever come up.

But in real life, and in professional practice, these are crucial considerations. The initial suggestion or advice is almost always an experimental procedure—as wisely constructed, to be sure, as possible. Nevertheless it is tentative, to be initiated and then followed up to evaluate its success and to be modified as necessary in light of the way it affects and is affected by the specific problem and people involved.

The solutions we will propose to problems will be tentative, for trying out. They will be proposed because they are logical and tested ways of solving the problems as given, but they are nevertheless always proposed only as worthy of trial, not positively as sure solutions.

They will require careful followup with the critical eye that an experiment calls for, to judge whether the direct results are satisfactory and the broader effects are acceptable. And instead of a sense of failure, inadequacy, or disappointment, the lack of satisfactory results should produce only a resolve to try a different or modified solution. A dozen solutions—or a hundred—might be proposed for the same situation, but any one which is carefully planned and executed from the principles described should offer good hope, because it also is a logical and tested way of solving the problem at hand.

We mean to convey, then, a sense of continuity in the way problems are attacked and solved, a flow of problem-solving effort that never ceases. The process truly flows from a problem's beginning to its end with hardly a notice, after a while, to what the first and last parts are. What matters is that the problem be solved, that you persist with your efforts until it is solved, that you always be able to generate new and reasonable efforts, and that you always give attention to the process until the problem is overcome.

The number of failures that occur en route to the solution, and the modifications that may be required, become largely irrelevant—provided that your efforts are not much less efficient than they could be with careful planning. What is most important is that reasonable efforts always be exerted until success is achieved.

Stating the Problem

We will not repeat here the problem-solving process described in detail in previous chapters. We will, however, be reemphasizing in this chapter some of the more important principles directly involved in handling common problems in training for self-discipline. Stating the problem clearly, for example, is the first step for finding solutions. This is not always simple to do, however. Often there are so many problems, or an initial statement of a problem is so confused, that the professional must spend considerable time with the parent trying to determine what to begin to work on.

The first problem we will be discussing, for instance, is bed-wetting, a simple and obvious enough difficulty to face and to solve. But the parent who presented it might have begun her counseling session by saying to the counselor; "I'm here because Charlie is such a bad boy." Or "Charlie just seems never to listen to me or to do what I tell him to." Or "That boy is impossible. He can't ever seem to listen to me or do what he is told to." Or "That boy is impossible. He can't ever seem to control himself." Or "My son has some nasty habits." Or "Charlie can't ever visit his friends or go to camp." Or "I'm worried because Charlie is so sensitive and withdrawn." Or "My boy has complexes."

The counselor—or the parent alone—would then have to try to specify a concrete, important problem of behavior that could be worked on and solved. The ways this would be done are probably obvious. Why is it that Charlie is called "such a bad boy"? What is his behavior that gives rise to such a description? If Charlie "seems never to listen" or to "do what he is told to," what is it that he is supposed to be listening to and doing? If he is "impossible" and unable to "control himself," what is his behavior that is so annoying or out of control? Or why can't he visit friends or go to camp? Or what is the behavior that leads the parent to worry about his sensitivity and withdrawal, and then what is it that makes him feel sensitive and withdrawn?

All these paths of questioning in this case would lead to the bed-wetting behavior—and, incidentally, often indicate consequences of failure of training and self-discipline in the habit of urinary control. The parent, then, once the problem is so defined, can proceed to institute the procedures we will be suggesting for this problem.

We will be starting with the *sufficient* description of a problem. By "sufficient" description, we mean nothing more than a description of behavior by the child that can be observed and changed—specific, direct, uninterpreted behavior. We do not mean vague or general *interpretation* of behavior, such as "impossible" or "sensitive" or "uncontrolled" or "complexes." Such terms represent a process of filtering through a feeling or theory that presents an indirect and subjective reaction of the parent, rather than an objective, directly observable kind of activity by the child.

Resources for Solutions

With the problem stated as simply and directly as possible, the parent will then need to consider details that will provide the leverage and materials for a solution. In the bed-wetting case, for example, who is around when the child prepares for bed, during the night when he may need to be awakened, and in the morning when he may need to be rewarded or penalized for his nighttime behavior? What rewards and penalties are most meaningful in his life? What sleeping arrangements can be made that will not bother others if the child must be awakened during the night or in the morning?

It is important that such resources be considered if success is to be insured. Often a parent or another child may interfere with the solution if his possible role with the child who has the problem is overlooked. In a positive way, enlisting the cooperation of such others in the child's life can increase the chances of success. A reasonable solution may fail, not because it is inappropriate, but simply because its application has not considered the total setting of the problem—the other people involved and the general household and family habits.

Some simple equipment may be necessary to put certain solutions into effect. Perhaps a lock on the door may be desirable to protect a child's room from the depredations of her brother. Perhaps an alarm clock will be desirable for the bed wetter. Perhaps the nonreading child should be provided with money to buy books that catch his fancy. If the expense is impossible in a poor family, an alternative can always be devised. We do not believe a large expense is ever necessary. An alarm clock can be bought at the Salvation Army, and used books are available at ten cents each.

Not even in the matter of rewards need expense be significant. Rewards can be almost anything of importance to the child. Best of all are the rewards *inherent in the achievement itself.* In the case of bed-wetting, the "rewards" of having no secret weakness to be ashamed of, of being able to visit a friend or go to camp without anxiety, or of being accepted as a maturing sufficient child instead of a handicapped one, can be and usually are the most satisfying gains possible. These intrinsic rewards may need to be pointed out to the troubled child, however, to give him hope and interest in solving the problem.

When, however, an *extrinsic* reward must be used, almost any agent meaningful to the child can be used. For staying dry, the mother's approbation may be sufficient, or the father's reading to the child before he goes to bed at night. Other rewards might be a desired item of clothing, a piece of sports equipment, a toy, money for a movie, a meal at a restaurant, a visit to the zoo. The enormous variety of extrinsic rewards is limited only by the parent's imagination. There is always *something* which will have impact upon the child.

Expectations for the course of the solution must be kept reasonable. Immediate, infallible, stable results should never be expected. One can hope for, indeed expect, some immediate results, but the achievement of a full, permanent solution may take a long time, or may, indeed, never be totally accomplished.

At first, for instance, the child who won't play with other children may play with just a child or two and for only brief periods. In fact, this would be a desirable way to proceed toward a solution—in small steps. The bed-wetting may be controlled for only a night or two at first. Then, gradually, the control—the self-discipline—can be extended to increasing lengths of time. And the child may lapse at times into a day of withdrawal from other children, or a night of bed-wetting. But the road to success can be clearly seen once a solution is launched, with modest but slowly increasing accomplishment.

If, however, the parent expects success at once and is impatient and disappointed about any failures or setbacks, he is not as likely to reinforce the positive movement that does occur, and thus he reduces the chances for eventual success.

Even if, for years, the son tends to withdraw at times of crisis, or to wet his bed, such problems, if he is generally sociable and with good urinary control, can fairly easily be accepted and covered up. It is the predominance of effective self-discipline and of one's goals that is important, not the invariability of success.

While impatience may be the more common problem, the rigid commitment to any one effort also can obstruct the discovery of a solution. Too much patience may indicate that the parent is wearing blinders against direct observation of the failures of an effort but feels she must stubbornly hang on to it and desperately hope it will eventually work. Perhaps the advice has been professional and very expensive. Perhaps the wife has had to fight with her husband to give it a trial. Perhaps she feels that if this effort fails there is no further hope.

A fair trial would be in terms of weeks, certainly not many months, and practically never for as much as a year without results that are obvious to others or that show up in objective measures and not just in the parent's often wish-fulfilling and hope-distorted judgments.

There need never be a lack of new solutions to try out that offer more hope than old ones because they can be devised to take into account the sources of past failures.

Sometimes, it is true, the effects of an effort to change behavior may be delayed—some of the effects, that is, certainly not all. The professional person who gives you advice—or the nonprofessional or you yourself—may reply to your doubts about progress with, "There, there, you just have to give it more time to work. It's been a long time building up; it can't be overcome immediately." When, then, should you decide whether you are on the right track? Even though it may take a long time to overcome a difficult long-term problem, it is also true that you can easily start off with an inefficient or hopeless effort at a solution, and then you truly might never find success.

How can you tell when you are on the right track? You can only tell if there are landmarks along a path indicating success, indicators of progress that you can directly observe even though a substantial solution is some weeks or months away. No one can properly assure you that you are on the best road unless there are some measures of this fact as you go along, which make sense to you. Otherwise how could you handle reasonably the fact that six professionals might each, with confidence, advise a different solution, and that it is extremely unlikely that each suggestion would work equally well?

Our Presentation of Problems and Solutions

The problems to be discussed in the next three chapters are divided by age. This has been done mainly for the convenience of the reader in checking on problems most similar to what he may be experiencing, and not because problems and their solutions are so different among age groups.

The theory, principles, and techniques we have discussed apply equally well (and have been applied equally well) to all age groups, including adults. It is obvious, however, that the exact nature of the most common problems does differ by age—and also the manner of solutions, agents, and rewards. We will not repeat our previous discussion of this issue, but only at this point invite the reader to observe for himself the repetitive structuring of the different problems to be described, and the manner of the solution.

Is such repetition justified? We believe that it is, on the grounds that the reader will probably gain most from finding problems, among the many discussed, that tap her experiences with her children, and from gaining a sense of the consistency of our approach by reading about its application in a wide variety of situations with the widest age range of children.

The dozen or so problems that we have selected for each age range represent the most common and troublesome we have observed in the literature and encountered in our clinical practices, but they have been selected also because they would seem to be the most useful to illustrate the techniques for the solution of practically any problems.

They have not been chosen exactly on the basis or order of their frequency in the general population. This book is not intended to serve as an encyclopedia of solutions to children's problems. It is meant to offer the more comprehensive service of helping to provide the attitudes and methods necessary to solve *any* problem that may arise.

The problems to be presented will serve, then, only to illustrate the rest of this book. If you do not find in this section the most important problem confronting you at the moment with your child, you should be able to find a problem sufficiently similar—and a solution sufficiently adaptable—to be of use.

Even when you find a problem very similar to one you face, you must treat the proposed solution as just one sketch of how you might proceed. It is far more important that you learn and apply the attitudes and principles of the rest of the book, than the trial solution precisely as it is suggested. It is also important that the adaptations you will almost surely have to make in the proposed solution, to fit your exact situation, not be contradictory to the principles discussed. As long as they are consistent with the principles, however, they can be varied greatly.

Suppose, for example, you are trying to get your child to go to bed, and stay there, at a reasonable hour. If you want to establish this behavior as a firm habit, you must not change this objective for a number of days (except for emergencies). Until it is well established, exceptions should not be made. That is a principle that should be held to rigorously. Another firm principle should be that you promise to reward this behavior and that you invariably do so during the training period.

What the reward is can be varied greatly according to your interests and what appeals to the child. For a young child, if may consist of being read to if he is in bed (and, the night before, stayed there) by a set time. Or he may be allowed to look at a late TV program on a weekend night.

Or he may be given money for a magazine or book he wants. An older child may be given use of the car, a prized piece of fishing tackle, or a piece of jewelry, for making a curfew.

The principles of effective training are what matter, and they are illustrated with just one of hundreds, perhaps thousands, of variations that are possible on a solution. In fact, you are unlikely to find any one of the proposed solutions the best one in all details for your purpose. There will almost surely be useful modifications you can make which will improve any solution in your particular situation.

CHAPTER XIII

Some Commonly Raised Questions, and Answers, Ages 2-6

THIS CHAPTER CONSISTS of a number of commonly raised questions, with trial solutions, about handling behavior and other problems among very young children. Some similar problems do occur at later ages and will in some cases be raised again, since specific forms and solutions will be different. Our focus here, then, will be on be on children ages two to six.

1. How can I get him to quit wetting the bed? Bed-wetting is common among preschoolers. It occurs most frequently among boys, perhaps four or five times more often than with girls. The peak years seem to be between age two (when you expect the child to begin self-control) and age five, although bed-wetting may persist throughout childhood, into adolescence, and even into adulthood—at declining rates.

Generally, a program of better control of the child's activities will help, if not wholly remedy, the bed-wetting: better order in his play and in his food and water intake at night; avoiding late TV shows, or pillow-fights that excite or anger the child.

The bed-wetter is often described as "a very sound sleeper," which probably means that he does not feel or notice internal cues that tell him he needs to void. A gentle, firm, and consistent program of getting him up at night at some appointed time (say, when the parents go to bed) or at some time shortly before his usual wetting time (if you know this—and you should observe so that you know if it is early during the night, or late, in the pre-morning hours) can be helpful.

These measures at least prevent the bed-wetting from going along unchallenged. As the routine of waking is established, at first by the parent's intervention, it can later be taken over by the child. Another useful measure is to set an alarm clock (an electric one that does not run down and thus complicate matters) a precautionary amount of time before the usual bed-wetting time. Before the alarm clock is set, let the child hear it a few times, get up out of bed to turn it off (keep it far enough from the bed so as to require him to get out of bed in order to turn it off), and practice, when he is wide awake, going to the bathroom. Then, during the night, when he has to perform this sequence, he is already familiar with it and can focus on the matter at hand, namely voiding in the toilet, not in bed.

Keeping a record of his performance can also be helpful—to the parent as well as the child. For each successful day, give him a "goody" of his liking; if he goes a week without a mishap, a larger reinforcement is indicated. A small desk calendar can suffice as a record-keeper, and the child should (if he is able) keep his own record. This helps to objectify the whole procedure and avoids scolding and making the child feel unsuccessful or guilty because of the parental attitude rather than the objective facts. Censure should be avoided; praise and direction-setting are far more useful.

Bed wetters do not get over their bad habit all at once.

It may take months, although some successes are achieved in a few weeks. Older children tend to take longer, probably because their poor habits are more firmly established and are related and tied to other behavior. Bed-wetting can often be self-punishing (preventing a child from staying overnight with friends or from going to scout or other camp-outs, for example), and usually damages the child's self-confidence, especially if the child is of school age or if others learn about it.

2. How can I get her to eat what she should? Eating problems are also common, and they seem to affect each sex about equally. Children's appetites tend to wax or wane considerably, from one day to another, or over even longer blocks of time. Parents become anxious that the child will not grow properly and, in fussing a good deal about this, create or aggravate psychological problems.

Also, many parents give their children too much to eat. This makes it easy for the child to refuse food. In fact, it may make it almost necessary, even for a healthy, reasonable child. Furthermore, nutritional balance may be sacrificed by insisting that the bulk of the food be eaten.

If a child is already somewhat stubborn because of other problems, he can take a stand against eating and no one can do much about it. It is an area of considerable self-control which the child can exercise against parental wishes and cajolery, and the parent can readily be the loser in the direct confrontation.

To remedy this problem, the parent can put on the child's plate very small amounts of all foods normally served and desirable at a meal, saying nothing. If the child eats it all, she can be complimented. If after a given period of time (say, 20 to 25 minutes) the food, or most of it, has not been eaten, the parent can quietly but firmly take away the plate and dismiss the child from the table—having told her ahead of time that this will be the procedure. No irregular meals (or access to the refrigerator, or other snacking) are to be allowed between times; only juice, fruit, or milk is to be available outside of regular meal times. (This assumes the child has no serious health problems. If she has, a physician should be consulted before any plan to overcome eating problems is pursued.) Parental actions should be consistent, meal after meal; verbal battles should be avoided, and crying and other forms of resistance should be ignored.

If a given type of food (say, a vegetable) is not liked or tried by the child, the parent may put some *small* amount of this type of food on the child's plate and when he has eaten it (or even taken a bite or two), other more desired food may be given and can operate as a reinforcer. Then the parent can go back to the vegetable and, bit by bit, cross over from the vegetable to the more wanted food until a reasonable portion of the vegetable has been eaten. This method can be extended, then, to other rejected but necessary foods, and the reinforcing food can be varied— none of us wants the same food all the time, even if he likes it.

Praise and encouragement are the hallmarks of the process of changing behavior. Avoiding verbal abuse, threats, and statements of hopelessness or exasperation is their corollary.

3. **How can I get him to play with the neighbor kids?** In answering this query, we are assuming that it is desirable for your child to play with the neighbor child (or to play more generally with peers). The problem is not as obvious as such problems as bed-wetting or eating, since the child may have other sources of social activity that are satisfactory, or may have limited but nevertheless reasonable social needs and desires.

Introducing the neighbor child and yours gradually is better than throwing them together and saying "Go play!"

Letting them meet via short conversations while with their parents, in a short car ride, or when the fathers are out working in the yard, may be a good introductory step.

Notice the playing skills of your child and of the other child. Are they markedly different? If so, the children may not be able to play together harmoniously to any extent. Introduce toys or play activities you think (or know) are liked by both children, and through some short-term supervision provide time for them to play together up to but not past the point where they get fatigued or irritable with one another. Young children do not play long at any one activity anyhow; variety is the main characteristic of their games. A bright five-year-old is not going to be challenged by play with a two-year-old; and a bright two-to-three-year old is going to require more stimulation in his play than a slow and unverbal five-year-old.

It is a good idea to get young children together on a picnic, at a lunch, during a brief ride to the store, or when there is enough going on to offer various content and levels of activity, and to observe how well the children get along. A small but good start can be built upon, whereas too long a time together at dull material can sour the children on each other, at least temporarily.

4. **How old should the child be to have jobs to do?** A very young child can help pick up his toys at the end of a play period; he can help his mother set the table by putting out unbreakable articles such as knives, forks, and spoons, plastic dishware, and napkins; and he can put his soiled clothes in the hamper. Many of these chores can be structured as games, and he can engage in the "helping" role so common among young children.

As the child gets older, he can do more tasks and more complex ones: hang up his clothes, straighten the room, bring in or take out groceries, bring in the newspaper or mail, help prepare foods, take responsibility for outside lawn work, and so on. There is enough to do in most households to give the child of any age some regular chores and responsibilities.

It should be clear to the reader by now that we emphasize the value of small but consistently held-to responsibilities. All of us have tasks we must do, regardless of whether we like them. Part of effective living requires that we do some undesirable tasks and not let them hang over us indefinitely in worrisome and debilitating ways. Some preparation for doing the necessary but thankless jobs, as well as the likeable ones, will make life easier and, in the long run, more satisfying for the child.

5.   **How can I get the child to put away his things?** This problem fits in with #4, above, in that putting away his things is another small task that can be integrated into the child's play activities. The child may be told before he gets out his toys that when his play period is over, or when his friend goes home, or when it is time for dinner (make the time limit as specific and intelligible to the child as possible), his toys will have to be put away. Sometimes a little start by the mother or father is helpful with the very young child. The parent then gradually fades out and leaves the rest (under a watchful eye) to the child.

Also, a child can be told that his next activity—eating, hearing a story, watching TV, or whatever—can begin only after he has put away his toys. You make something he wants contingent on his finishing a task, or carrying out a chore. This is a gentle, firm, and consistent way of managing many situations that would otherwise be likely to end up in a fight or impasse with the child.

6.   **Should I put my child in nursery school?** Although this is a difficult question to answer satisfactorily without having many details about the particular child's parent's situation, some general considerations can be discussed. One, does the child need companions of his

own age? Two, is the child too dependent upon family members (especially on adults or much older siblings)? Three, is the nursery school well recommended by people of discrimination and intelligence? Four, have you and the child visited several perspective nursery schools and approved firsthand what the general situation is at one or more (such as size, composition of group, impressions about the teacher, interaction with a friend who has a child in the school)? Costs, length of day, transportation, and availability of kindergarten and first grade in the same setting may also be important considerations.

If you are in serious doubt after you have looked into all relevant factors, you may try to enroll the child for a limited period of time. Don't just put the child in the school and hope for the best without preparing yourself and the child as fully as you can. A limited trial period may be set by the school itself—say a month or two—but you may want to consider a special arrangement such as a summer term or a half-day session for a semester.

Avoid grilling the child on whether he likes the nursery school. Most children will spontaneously tell you in subtle ways how they react to school. Keep your eyes and ears open and observe what he says; and, of course, you can always ask the teacher for her observations and advice after a trial period.

While readiness in a general sense is probably important, the idea can easily be overworked. A child can be ready for broader experiences at *any* time in his life (as can adults), but the real issue is whether the nursery school is the best place and way for the child to spend his time, whether it is set at his level, whether alternative schools are better, and, as with any other purchase of service, whether it provides good value for the effort and money that will be required.

Some gradual preparation may be useful. Visits, as we have already mentioned, are useful to introduce the child to the school and to the routine; perhaps an hour's visit or two before full enrollment would be desirable. Some picture and story books about nursery schools might also help. And, of course, the experiences related by older siblings, neighboring children, or relatives can also be useful introductions and guides.

7. **What should I do if she cries when we go out at night?** One theme that is repeated often in this kind of situation is that of "Parting is such sweet sorrow." The child and the parent both feel overwrought, and there often is crying, promising, cajolery, scolding, and even punishment. Usually none of these dramatics is of any use, and often they make the problem worse.

Avoiding emotional displays is important. Let the child know you are going out a little before you go (perhaps when the baby-sitter is expected); then try to treat his protests as matter-of-factly as possible. You cannot answer the upset effectively with words—you can usually handle it best with calm, consistent, and reasonable deeds. Don't try to play tricks on the child, such as slipping out, telling him you will be right back and then not coming back, or other subterfuges. Be candid. Yes, you are going out—and he can have a story read to him, or can play games with the baby-sitter, or can watch a desired program on TV, by way of a pleasant activity following your departure. You then point to what the child can do that is interesting and enjoyable, not to what you are doing.

Your activities should really not be open to questions, or only rarely. You would be training the child very poorly if you let her dictate your social life at such times. Be sure, of course, that what you want is reasonable, that you are gently and firmly going to act in such and such a way, and that the child's attention is focused on what his alternatives are, not on cajolery, punishment, or a kind of blackmail exacting some unreasonable sense of guilt on your part.

After the evening is over, do not say, "See, you were all

right with Maggie [the sitter]. Aren't you ashamed of your crying last night?" Let the matter drop. The only time to introduce it is the next time you plan to go out at night, and then only to do the firm, fair, and consistent thing again.

Sometimes going out briefly during the daytime can introduce the child to your absence and she can get used to it. Or you can leave her in the yard to play (depending upon her age) while you step into the neighbor's house for a short visit, or you can go into the store to shop awhile, leaving her in the car—preferably with another person. There are a number of small ways you can acquaint her with the idea of your absence. The main idea is for *you* to accept and plan reasonably for the fact that you will be away; the child will soon get used to it, because you will act wisely and firmly on this premise.

8. **What if he is mean to his baby-sitter?** The baby-sitter should have instructions on how to handle your child, especially if there are any questions of importance. If medicine is to be given, this is obviously important and to be followed. It is also important, however, that if a given bedtime is to be observed, the sitter should enforce it, and if the child is supposed to help (depending upon his age) with some chores, the baby-sitter should be fully aware of and follow up on these responsibilities. The baby-sitter, then, should be cued in on what you expect from the child and from the sitter. Written regulations, times, and procedures are very useful in such situations, at least until the sitter gets used to your family routine. It is all the more important if you have more than one child to be cared for in this way.

If the baby-sitter is very young, immature, or inexperienced, your child may sense this and try to "get away with murder," including being unkind, discourteous, or generally difficult with the sitter. A child senses when he can get his way, or when he is likely to win in conflict—the more so when the authority figure is doubtful of her authority. Just scolding the child will do no good; nor will the sitter's threats or later punishments. The best way to handle conflict between the sitter and your child is to set the structure yourself, to say in the presence of both of them that the child may do so-and-so (such as having a story read or watching TV) between such-and-such times (if the child can comprehend time), and then he is to go to bed. Details such as leaving a light on, keeping the radio going, or having a favorite doll or toy in bed should all be spelled out in advance. If there is no structure here, the child will have opportunity to exceed every limit and take any advantage open, in a contest of wills. The sitter should be told to be firm and to take down notes of what happened, how, and why, while this situation remains a problem, so you can extend your efforts to solve the situation through any reasonable means. The sitter is acting for you, the parent, in your absence and should have the authority to manage the child as you indicate. Sometimes sitters can be better managers than the parents themselves!

9. **What if he is afraid of the dark?** Fear of the dark is common among young children. It is, in a sense, "natural," in that the child has to get used to facing the unknown (something a lot of adults also have trouble with), and to knowing that within the darkness there is no threat to his welfare. Moreover, this learning should provide the confidence that comes with knowing that he can turn on the light and dispel the darkness (or the unknown).

To help the child overcome this fear (or prevent it, which is even better) you may go with him to new places (such as the basement or attic), showing him where to find the light, or how to open a troublesome door, or how the floor squeaks and how funny it sounds. He can go part of the way alone, with you standing on guard, and you can reassure him and compliment him on his mastery of the task. One can thereby usher the child from fear through some acquaintance with the situation, on to mastery through control of it.

Once you have helped the child through the reluctance, you can put him through the exercise occasionally so as to prevent his losing his calm and to upgrade his control of the situation. You can praise him for helping you, and leave out any reference to fear or reluctance once he has begun to perform well in this kind of situation.

Any kind of fear-provoking situation can be approached in this gradual manner, with your sustaining support and with your approval of his accomplishment, together with enough follow-through on later occasions to cement the growth and change he has shown.

10. **How can I get them to quit fighting all the time?** Almost all siblings fight sometime. You probably did with your brothers or sisters when you were a child (and may still do so!). Such fighting is common and natural, as a response to frustration or desire for mastery over person or situation. Fighting is an expression of anger, resentment, humiliation, or defeat. We all experience these emotions, including the child. Children close in age tend to fight more.

Although it is common, we wish to help the child overcome the excessive amount of fighting with peers or siblings that sometimes occurs. Several ideas may be of value to you, depending upon your situation.

First, try to separate the children at the time when they are most likely to fight. This may be at mealtime, early in the morning before breakfast, after dinner in the evening, before bedtime (when they are tired and irritable), or when traveling in the car together without much to do. Be alert to these fighting times and get ready for them— separate the children, give them different jobs to do, or help them pursue different leisure activities such as reading or watching TV.

Second, avoid fighting in reaction to their upsets. You will not teach them peaceful alternatives by being belligerent yourself. Your example is likely to be more potent than your words.

Third, give them advance notice that fighting will cause them to lose a cherished "goody," such as a dessert at mealtime, a story at the end of day, or some favorite TV-watching. You should put it positively, however: *"If you want your dessert, there will have to be no fighting."* Often these words, spoken firmly and supported by action, will be enough, after an application or two, to bring the desired behavior under control. An occasional reinstatement of your firmness will do much to maintain the newly developed control.

Fourth, don't try to find out whose fault the fighting is. You seldom can, so why complicate the situation? It is not usually important, anyhow—unless one child is really a bully. After all, you want to stop the fighting and redirect their energies, not to establish a court of law to find guilt and render justice. You need to solve the problem, as directly as possible.

Fifth, reward them generously when they behave well. Don't give attention only when there are misdeeds or problems. Let them know you appreciate their better behavior and self-control, with an extra helping of ice cream or an additional story or TV show.

11. **Am I giving her enough love?** This is a very hard question to answer in the abstract. You might as well ask, "Do I get enough vitamins in my meals?" One could not give a reasonable answer without knowing the details of your eating habits. However, the question of love arises because many parents feel guilty if their child has a problem, believing that problems reflect parental misdeeds, rejection of the child, carelessness, or insensitivity. As a

generalization, this is nonsense. All children have problems—all adults do, also. To think that the child's problems arise automatically because someone did not love him enough not only is erroneous and time-wasting, but does not lead to any useful solutions.

Most parents love their children, although when the child is misbehaving, most of us suspend the overt display of affection, quite naturally in most instances. You do not withhold love forever; but you do not warm up to anyone who is annoying you or causing disturbance. To do so would only reinforce the very misbehavior you are trying to overcome.

You do not have to express love to the child at all times or guard against expressing dislike for his misbehavior. Words are not *that* important if your general stance is warm and accepting, yet making room for disagreement, correction, and the withholding of common rewards.

If you think you handle problems wrong, and feel guilty about it, the best remedy is to correct the child's behavior that is in question. Just feeling guilty about it and trying to assuage your apprehensions with excessive displays of love will not help much. It is better to get to the source—your behavior relative to the child's misbehavior.

12. **What if he is always asking me what to do?** If the child is dependent upon you to decide his actions and directions, you have probably acted in ways to make him look to you excessively and to mistrust himself. You will want to shore up his decision-making and action-taking potential.

You can do several things. First, throw the question back to him: "What are your choices?" Second, do not be put in the position of having actually to come up with answers—let him do that. You can then reinforce a good answer you think deserves credit; if there is none, to make no reply is all right. Third, think in advance as to when the child might be at loose ends—when other children are away at holiday or vacation time, when colds keep him indoors for several days, when others seem more socially resourceful—and give him special encouragement.

Try to figure out what you think leads to the child's lack of direction. If it is a need for opportunity to decide for himself, then that should be developed. If it is social skills, reread our chapters on this topic. If it is a temporary state due to illness, perhaps suggest pleasing activities (not too trying) that he must choose among (suggest alternatives, not the exact activity). If it is due to a trip and he is bored in the car with long drives, some new toys or games may be available as resources he must decide about. Try to provide alternatives from which selections may be made by him, thereby leading him into the decision-making and action-taking process.

If there is truly nothing the child wants to do—owing perhaps to temporary fatigue, anger, or sleepiness—then let the matter rest there. When the mood passes, as it surely will, the time for action will come and the child can be further trained as suggested. A child is seldom bored for long (given fairly free rein) unless the boredom is constantly reinforced by adult intervention.

CHAPTER XIV

Some Commonly Raised Questions, and Answers, Ages 7-12

PROBLEMS OF CHILDREN seven to twelve years old are the focus of this chapter. The development of character, skills, and values requires special attention to preparing the child for the self-control and self-imposed standards he will need to act independently in adolescence and adulthood. The *principles* of training remain the same as in the earlier period, but because behavior is now more varied and complex, the parent must make a special effort to isolate the small segments that are most accessible to her (or his) control and that will contribute to larger changes which cannot be accomplished directly. Otherwise the parent may feel confused or overwhelmed by the increasing complications in the child's behavior. She also must try to avoid being distracted by the child's verbal behavior and neglecting what the child is actually doing—in other words, she must not to let words mask the nature of the situation or behavior that needs changing.

1. **Should I make my child learn to play a musical instrument?** Parents naturally want their children to develop skills, and it is a theme of this book that

helping children to develop competence contributes greatly to their satisfaction with their lives. It is a question here of goals—whether skill specifically with a musical instrument is the most desirable choice of a goal for attention. The first question to be raised, then, is what other skills might be developed, and which to choose. The highest priority in making the choice should be given to the child's abilities and interests, so that the skill chosen is the one that most likely can be carried the farthest among the various possibilities, and with the child's maximum interest.

It should not be a question of *whether* the child has any abilities and interests, however, but *which* alternative to choose. The parent can perhaps best prepare the child to contribute to the decision by exposing her (or him) to as wide a variety of cultural and recreational activities as possible, and observing results closely. The child can thus develop or demonstrate ability and interest on which to build. It would certainly not be wise for the parent arbitrarily and without such experimentation to assign the child to piano lessons when the child might have more liking and potential for painting, swimming, tinkering with mechanical things, or studying birds. If the child, having been exposed to a wide variety of possibilities, still shows no special interests or aptitudes, it is time enough for the parent to make a choice arbitrarily (or according to such practical considerations as availability of a good teacher, the parent's skill in something which he can help the child with, or handy facilities for this or that) and to assign the child the task of developing, at least experimentally, her skills in a particular field.

Once the choice is made, some trial period might be set, at the end of which child, parent, and teacher would evaluate the child's progress and interest and try to determine whether further training is desirable or whether experimentation with another field might be wiser.

During the trial period, some structure of practicing and reinforcement should be set which will be developing self-discipline as well as skill in the child. Practice periods should be brief, rigorously adhered to, and followed by rewards such as a prized TV program, a demonstration before an attentive audience (of one, if necessary), a desired snack, even a small present now and then, such as an appealing book or magazine, a key ring, or a pocket notebook, which might also be reinforcing of other desirable habits. The parent can also offer opportunities that make presence of the budding skill inherently rewarding to the child. For example, if she wishes, she might be permitted to invite her friends for a little party for which she plays, or to have a fun session within the family by having the father play some other instrument with her or having her play background music for a home movie or slide show.

2. **What should I do when he talks back?** There is no inherently best way to train the child with regard to "talking back." Parents themselves differ widely in their own "talking back" patterns, and their own example and wishes may be the most important influence on the child. The most rational approach would probably be for the parents to require the child to act the way they themselves behave in this regard. Thus parents would have to be careful that they did not brawl with each other, or talk roughly to the child, if they did not want the child to talk back in kind. What you are training the child to do may be determined more by your behavior than by your instructions or intentions.

Assuming, however, that you do not want your child to "talk back" in nasty, obscene, or discourteous ways, you should insure that he is not learning these very ways from more powerful influences in the home than are discouraging the behavior. Also you should make sure that he has adequate opportunities and channels to express disagreement in other, acceptable ways that are encouraged and rewarded more than "talking back"—alternative ways to make himself heard and influential.

You should be sure that you are not listening to him, getting involved with him, and making concessions only when he "talks back," as a way of getting rid of him and his mouthiness, and that you are not ignoring him, or paying minimal attention, or not really making concessions even when his case is reasonable, if he speaks up more politely or moderately.

Once, then, you decide upon your goal, and make sure that you are illustrating the means you want him to follow, you should try very hard to ignore or isolate him when he tries to browbeat you verbally to get his way. If you concede to him when he is "mouthy," you will be rewarding and reinforcing that kind of behavior, no matter how much abuse you heap on him while making the concession. Your words of objection just won't be as important as what you give him of what he is demanding.

Contrariwise, then, you should try very hard to reward the more courteous ways you want him to adopt, by trying to make your concessions at that time and only then. Of course, you should not fulfill unreasonable requests merely because he is courteous. Too often, children are trained to expect anything they want just because they speak politely; courtesy alone in their behavior may be emphasized and rewarded at the expense of values and character.

3. **What should I do when she says she is too sick to go to school and I don't believe it?** When the child claims to be too sick to go to school, it is necessary to determine whether this is organically true. The vital importance of determining this as well as possible *in all instances* lies in the fact that if, even just once or twice,

she is able to avoid school because of a false claim, this escape route from unpleasant situations is reinforced and more likely to occur again. Of course it is often difficult to be sure of physical sickness, particularly at its onset; physicians are difficult to reach and costly to consult for all ailments and even they are often unsure and may have their own interests to consider. They may, for example, prefer to keep a child home rather than take a chance that the sickness may show up later (thus ignoring or making secondary the problem of reinforcing malingering). But it is usually the parent, with expert help when reasonable, who must make a judgment of likely physical versus psychological causes by consulting with the teacher, asking classmates about any classroom trouble, and listening to any clues the child may provide in her conversation or other behavior.

When, in the parent's best judgment, the child seems most likely to be "faking" sickness (even though, possibly, the child is unaware that she is doing this) and the chances of serious physical disease are very low, and when there will be sufficient time and opportunity later to pick up additional physical symptoms if they become serious, the parent must be prepared to do whatever is necessary to get the child back to school.

At this point another judgment might also be considered. Are conditions at school bad enough so that the parent should intervene to try to modify whatever the situation is that may be bringing on the faked sickness? Or is the school situation such that the child should try to learn to cope with it on her own? In general we favor the latter course, since, if the child is to be able to progress reasonably well through school (as well as in life), she will have to learn how to handle adverse conditions—whether heckling classmates, a nagging teacher, vague assignments, arbitrary grades, or some other problem. But there are times also when the parent should intervene either directly or through the teacher to try to modify a situation which is very unusual and beyond the capacity of even a reasonably adequate child to deal with.

Having considered all the evidence, including discussion with the child, the parent should make a firm decision and then stick with it despite whatever fuss the child makes. Otherwise the parent would be rewarding the fussing. The situation can get heart-rending as the child cries and pleads for mercy, insists that she feels desperately ill, accuses you of cruelty. But having made your decision as wisely as possible, you must be obdurate. Your payoff will come when, if you are correct in your judgment, your child's tendency to feign illness in order to get out of school will lessen and finally disappear, unless a more overwhelming situation arises. If you are incorrect, you should learn how more likely to be correct in the future; that is crucial in our whole procedure. The same principle applies to dental visits, doing household tasks, attending new groups, and the like.

You really do not have the choice between playing it safe about physical illness or not playing it safe. At least it is far more meaningful in terms of dealing with your child in the future to view the problem as one of either rewarding the tendency to use physical complaints to get out of unpleasant situations, thus making the tendency stronger for the future, or not rewarding the tendency, thus reducing the likelihood of its occurring in the future.

4.   **How can I get her to go to bed?** Structuring the bedtime situation is very important if, and only if, the parent is upset when the child does not go to bed expeditiously when asked to. The conversation between them as they argue, or the child's obvious procrastination about complying, then produces the problem for the parent. Some parents are not bothered by the child's bedtime habits, whatever time within reason she gets to

bed, if she maintains good health. They leave the child to her own devices. Once parents ask or demand a certain reasonable bedtime deadline, however, they should see to it that their words have meaning, by enforcing whatever the words require of the child.

How, then, can the parent go about insuring that the child will be in bed at the appointed hour? First of all, the deadline should be coordinated with such considerations as the child's health, family mealtimes, sibling habits, and necessary preparations in the bathroom, with as little modification as possible. Then meaningful rewards should be provided if the deadline is met. The father will read to the child for ten minutes if the child is in bed as scheduled, or the child can have a new book to read, or she can look at a TV program for a short time or have a special snack. Balkiness and delay past the deadline should mean, without exception, that the reward is withheld for that night, no matter what fuss is raised, but that it can be earned the next night. If the parent stands firm, perhaps sometimes modifying the rewards if she believes that there are more appealing but still reasonable ones available, she can expect that, after a night or two or three as the child acclimates to the parent's firmness, to the process of getting ready, and to the desirability of earning the reward, she will usually succeed in her purpose.

5. **How can I teach him the value of money?** You can best teach the value of money—in whatever form you want him to learn it—by conducting your financial business with him in the way you want him to learn. This is to assume, of course, that you are first clear in your mind as to what you want him to learn about money. This is to assume also that you *want* him to learn about money affairs as they are really conducted in the world and will try to keep as consistent about this as possible.

For example, you cannot expect to teach your child the

conventional value of money if you do not want to pay him for his tasks around the house because, you believe, he should do them for glory alone or for social values rather than for pay. What, then, *should* he be paid for, if not for the work he does? And what kind of rewards are you going to put ahead of money, in this instance? And how else is he supposed to "learn the value of money" as you presumably want him to? It is practically impossible for him to learn the value of money in any conventional sense that he can live by as an adult, if you simply give him his money when you feel like it and in any amounts you wish. He may then perhaps be taught how to spend it well—but surely not how to earn it and to value it in view of the difficulty in coming by it.

To learn the value of money, then, the child must have a chance to earn it, beginning at the youngest age at which he can perform any useful services around the house, and be paid a reasonable amount for it at least weekly so that the rewards come soon enough to be anticipated. You must also be sure that the money is truly a reward because the child (like the adult) can exchange it for something he appreciates. It is meaningless, for example, for the parent to require the child to put any substantial part of the money he earns into the bank or investments, for his college education, or even for next year's camping trip. A year ahead, much less ten or fifteen years, is far too distant to make the money seem worthwhile for a seven- or twelve-year old to work for.

6. **How can I keep relatives from spoiling her?** The problem of keeping relatives—or anyone else—from spoiling your daughter or son can be handled from either or both of two directions: by trying to control or instruct the offending relative, or by trying to train the child in how to cope with such a tempting but presumably harmful situation.

The most difficult approach would be to try to train your daughter's grandmother or aunt in how to treat your daughter. You will probably be told that a little indulging won't hurt the child, or hear it implied that you are mean in denying the child and relative this pleasure. In any case you would be taking on the toughest way to handle the problem by trying to control the indulgence through bearing down on the relative and trying to straighten her out. You will have enough trouble trying to train those much more subject to your influence in time and proximity.

It is only slightly less difficult to try to teach your child how to take the same disapproving attitude toward the relative as you take. You may *wish* that your daughter would say to Grandma, "No, thanks, I'm not supposed to eat candy before meals," or "I'm not allowed to stay up till midnight watching television." To ask this of your young child, however, is to put too heavy a burden of responsibility on her—perhaps merely to relieve yourself of doing the job. Any seven-to-twelve-year-old who can accept and apply your restrictive rules in turning down the offers of another respected adult such as a grandmother or aunt is likely to be either supermature or superafraid of you. The one is too much to expect; the other would be at the expense of self-development.

The two generally more effective methods of keeping the child from being spoiled by relatives involve controlling either the child or the exposure to relatives. The positive training in discipline you can provide by following the principles of this book will be the best antidote to occasional exposure to spoiling. The rare episode will seldom harm well-established habits. Your best approach will probably be to insure that the situations for spoiling are under your control either by asserting your own rules and influence over any indulging the relatives may want to do, or by simply not permitting the child to be exposed to spoiling situations more than you and she can handle easily.

Exceptions to your rules in training the child—which is, after all, what episodes of "spoiling" are—will not harm your training or the child's increasing self-discipline, *if* the rules are well-established. It is the same with any habit and exceptions to it. And the value of the indulgence for the relationship between child and relative may even make it worthwhile—occasionally. But when the "spoiling" disrupts the habits you are trying to establish, it will be up to you to step in and eliminate the exceptions, either by overruling what the relative is doing with your child or by forbidding your child to accept the relative's indulgence. This may expose you to criticism from others, but your alternative is to face more trying experiences with your child—and chances are that your relationship with your child is the far more important one in determining your satisfaction with your life.

7.   **What if my husband (wife) won't cooperate in the discipline effort?** In the training effort with the child, it is best, of course, to gain the cooperation of as many of the people influencing the child as possible, especially those in the immediate household. This would include the other children as well as both parents in such instances, for example, as teaching the child not to bully *anyone*, parent or sibling, by alerting everyone to observe and penalize it immediately; or not allowing any stealing from anyone, by alerting all household members to it and having them lock up money or penalize promptly any thefts. *How* to obtain the cooperation of all possible positive forces in the training of the child is a separate topic, but it is usually possible to obtain it, especially from parents, if the situation is handled flexibly and imaginatively. Here, however, we are discussing the particular situation where,

despite reasonable efforts, the cooperation of your husband (or wife) seemingly cannot be obtained for a joint, consistent effort in some disciplinary regard.

In such a noncooperative situation, at least two conditions must be insisted upon for the training to be effective: that either you or your spouse be given the go-ahead to do the disciplining alone, and that the noncooperating parent not interfere with what the active parent is doing. Training cannot be effective where neither parent takes the lead to indicate what is expected and how it is to be performed, to observe whether it is done, and to reward (or penalize) appropriately. As in many other household situations, one parent may want or be willing to take the lead but be afraid of criticism from the inactive parent for whatever he or she does. And the parent who is unwilling to take part in the training but nevertheless persists in sniping at what his wife or husband tried to do, or encourages the child to resist the training, or even "makes up" to the child for his mother's or father's "mean" treatment or comforts the child when he is supposed to be suffering penalties, is quite likely to sabotage the training effort.

Given acceptance of the two rules—allowing the one parent to do what is necessary, and not undercutting the reward and penalty process—the active parent can proceed even if the other parent is noncooperative. It is this way in almost all problems of living. While it is always easier to accomplish goals if all forces involved are willing to cooperate, one should not use noncooperation as an excuse for not trying to solve problems. Seldom are both parents equally concerned and equally involved in any training problem with their children.

8. **Should children always have their own rooms?**
The problem of whether the child should have her own

room cannot be divorced from the family's economic condition. The answer must be that most families in the United States simply cannot provide a separate room for all the children in a large family. In small families, however, and in families with sufficient means to pick spacious homes or apartments, the problem becomes one of how best to spend the housing money—whether for separate rooms for the children or for larger shared living quarters such as recreation, dining, and living rooms.

No one really knows the exact housing circumstances under which children thrive best. Is it living communally, with a minimum of privacy, or is it having a space of their own that they can care for and be alone in when desired? Different housing circumstances undoubtedly develop different habits, and the least one might say is that *if* the parent values and wants *above all* to help the child to learn how to live comfortably with others, then she should encourage communal living quarters in the home. If, on the other hand, she wants *primarily* to encourage individualism in all habits and nonconforming development, perhaps private space should be provided.

Where the answers are so unclear and the goals so difficult to define, perhaps a compromise is the most comfortable way for most parents. That might be to provide a very small private space for sleeping, for privacy when wanted, and for a few personal possessions, but to make the shared space larger and more attractive, partly to encourage communal living within the family and partly because it is a more economical use of the limited space and money for housing.

No parent need feel guilty about not providing a private room when that is not practical. It is best for the child to grow up living with and appreciating the economic realities of the family situation. Furthermore, not enough is known about what the best housing arrangement is. Perhaps it is best to let what is most apparent and practical determine how the space in the house is used. That is, if a child sleeps poorly in the room with others, and better alone, he can be provided with a private sleeping space. Or if a young child is constantly bullied by an older one with whom he shares a room, or an older one is being annoyed by the habits or interference of a younger one when he needs to concentrate, it is time to try to provide private quarters.

9. **How can I get my child to be more sociable?** When you are concerned that the child is not sociable enough, you need to ask yourself how much is "enough" and what opportunities the child has to socialize with appropriate companions. How much is enough is too often determined by the parent's own worry that she (or he) is not "popular enough" and concern that the child should not feel that way. Or the parent may be disturbed because the child does not seem anxious enough about not being more sociable.

Really, given the enormous range of sociability that exists in both happy and unhappy adults—many adults are miserable despite numerous friends, and many are quite satisified with two or three friends—there is no single criterion for how much is enough. What you need to be concerned about is the overall satisfaction that the child has with her life, or symptoms of misery. If the child is contented with a very few friends and shows no signs of acute unhappiness, it is quite likely that her present level of friendships and mixing is adequate—and may continue to be adequate for the indefinite future. To impose some external standards on the child by saying that she does not have as many friends as so-and-so, or that she must be unhappy (as perhaps her mother was) because she does not seem to be popular, is to burden the child unnecessarily with some of the superficial criteria that made or make the parent feel like a social failure.

The opportunities that the child may have for socializing may also determine greatly, particularly at the younger ages of this group, how much mixing she does. At age seven, eight, or nine the child still does not have much opportunity to move around outside of the neighborhood (as she will when older). She may therefore be dependent for friendships on whether children her age happen to live nearby. If there are no congenial children at hand, the parent can help the situation by trying to bring in or to visit the children of friends, taking the child to playgrounds or community centers that are not otherwise accessible, or locating and encouraging the child to attend the meetings of groups that might interest him.

One caution: Children will almost inevitably gravitate for friendships to other children of their age, or if they are exceptional, to children of similar mental age or interests. Children who seem to get along better with or prefer the company of adults rather than companions their own age may need help to find playmates their age, or may be getting too much encouragement and reward from their parents for preferring the company of adults. Relating primarily or only to adults may contribute to habits in the child which will interfere with relationships with equals or cause their neglect. It may be very tempting for the parent to want the child with her when she does her work, when she entertains, when adult friends are around. Yet the bulk of the child's personal life will be spent with equals in age and status, and the habits learned in getting along with adults will be of only limited use in learning how to get satisfaction with peers. After all, adults will not usually heckle or bully children, will not usually "egg them on" to rebelliousness, will not applaud foolhardy acts, will compliment them for courtesy and conformity. An entirely different kind of behavior is required with peers.

10. **What should we do if he takes money from my purse or the house?** Too often the parent who gets upset about a child's stealing money from the mother's purse, father's wallet, or sibling's room takes a strictly

moralistic attitude toward the theft and overlooks the rewards that the child may obtain from stealing. Lecturing the child on his dishonesty, while it may make him feel guilty about what he did and may be worth doing to establish the parent's unequivocal attitude, should be abandoned if it does not curb the deed. If such admonishments do little or no good, it is quite likely that the child is getting rewards which, in his living habits, make it worthwhile to steal despite scoldings.

Chances are that his rewards—which maintain the stealing habit—are of either or both of two kinds: he is getting back at the parent or sibling for some resented treatment; or he is enjoying spending the money, either because companions like him for it or because he enjoys what he can buy. Parental control of this habit can take any of several forms. Above all, however, the child must not be allowed to profit from the stealing.

The parent should be alert to the loss of money from the house, and should take precautions to reduce the temptation to steal in the first place. Wallets, purses, and loose money should not be left accessible to the child with this bad habit. You may think that the child should learn to master this temptation rather than not be exposed to it. It offends many parents to have to put away money in their own home; they may do this when strangers are present, but do not think they should have to do so when just family is about. Still, it is a practical problem. One can look upon putting it away as making it easier for the child to develop good habits about it. That is, during the time you are trying to train him not to steal, you reduce the temptation, thus making it easier for him to learn how to earn and save money for what he wants. Once the habit of honesty with money is better established, you can presumably trust him better when it is left about.

If the child manages to steal anyway, the parent should watch for the rewards of the theft in terms of good times or objects purchased, question the child about the source of the money, and, if evidence accumulates which makes the explanation unsatisfactory and thieving likely, block opportunities to spend the money taken. Furthermore, if stealing can be reasonably proven as the source of the money used for the purchasing, the parent should insist upon restitution, either by returning the goods or by work to restore the money taken. Again, it is most important to remember that the child should not be permitted to profit from his misdeeds.

A preventive course is also open and should be pursued. The parent should make sure that he provides the child with a reasonable allowance or opportunity to earn money, on a regular basis, preferably weekly, with a regular pay time that the child can count on. Thus the child will have the chance to count on getting money. He also should be able to spend it as he wishes. It invites trouble either to provide no money at all to the child this age or to provide it only at the parent's whim in a way that the child has no control over. Yet many situations of stealing arise exactly in such a context—where money is simply not available in any way other than by stealing.

One final caution: The parent should be sure of his own habits of honesty regarding money if he wishes to train his child well. He should not shake out the children's piggy banks arbitrarily, take money secretly from his wife's purse (or she from his wallet), or describe how he cheated a tradesman out of a fair price. A parent's behavior is often justifiably more impressive to the child than mere words that the parent may mouth.

11. How can I keep him from bullying the younger children? You must assure as far as possible that bullying is not rewarding to the child, that he is not getting satisfying attention or reaction for it, that he is not getting the objects or privileges he wants from the younger children, that his punishment for doing the bullying is not merely nagging words or shouted words or threatening words that are never followed by action from you.

Nor do you want to reward the younger child for complaining all the time, unnecessarily or even unfairly. You must try, as much as you can, to be a firsthand observer of how the bullying arises and proceeds. If it is the most direct route taken to get something from the younger child, you should block its success in any reasonable way you can, looking to its goal rather than to the method. That is, instead of yelling at the offending child, or hitting him, or nagging him for grabbing something from the younger one or hitting the younger one to make him move or fetch something, you should forbid the younger child to comply with the bully, or otherwise forcefully block the bully from gaining his goal.

Once you can observe and block the purpose of the bullying and stop the bully from gaining his reward, you can try to redirect him to his object by suggesting acceptable ways he can obtain it—as by barter, persuasion, courtesy, or whatever other methods you wish him to learn to use to gain his ends.

You can enlist the other children to help block the bully. That is, if several children, even younger ones, unite to try to block the bullying, they may be able to succeed better than the lone victim. And your husband (wife) can be alerted to observe and handle the bullying behavior the same way that you are trying to do it.

12. **How can I get him to eat breakfast before he goes to school?** This is an elusive, nagging problem at all ages—including that of parents themselves, as observed in the father who grabs at a piece of toast and a gulp of coffee as he leaves the kitchen late to get to work. It is partly a problem of scheduling and partly a problem of no pressing hunger. Unlike at lunch and supper, one is often

not hungry at breakfast time, and eats primarily as a preventive measure (which the young child cannot easily learn so far ahead) to avoid later hunger.

One can attack the problem in two ways. The mother (usually) can move the early morning schedule along so that the child gets up in enough time and, until she develops strong enough habits, is monitored sufficiently to have time for a somewhat leisurely breakfast. And then breakfast, more than the other meals, when hunger is more acute, can be approached more as a luxury and pleasure than as a necessity. As firmly as possible, through the methods of scheduling, goal-setting, rewards, and penalties, the habit should be established of having the child sit down for breakfast at a regular time each morning, with a sufficient period to pursue the meal leisurely. This of course is an ideal that may never be completely reached, considering the trouble many people often have in functioning well first thing in the morning, parents and children, and the emergencies that come up about missing clothes, ride arrangements, physical complaints, unfinished assignments, and such. But one should approximate the definite and sufficient time period as best one can.

The breakfast menu should be given some special consideration, not for fancy cooking at such an hour, but for special delectability—rather than depending upon exhortation about how important it is to start the day off right, in face of the fact that the child is not hungry, or may be tense or nauseated, and in no mood to be persuaded of his long-term welfare.

13. **How can I get her to be less nervous?** To help a child get over "nervousness," you first have to decide exactly what habits you mean to include. Do you mean "nervousness" as shown by restlessness, scratching, tapping her foot, biting her nails, talking all the time, jumping up and down—or what? If it is a very limited habit such as

nail-biting alone, or foot-tapping, you should perhaps check first to determine whether the habit is observed only by you, either because you are too sensitive to it or because the child does it only in your presence or because it is a very private habit which only you are close enough to the child to observe. In any of these cases, you could perhaps learn to get over your concern instead of labeling it as the child's problem—if it exists with no other symptoms and has no implications for other behavior.

All we will be concerned about here and call "nervousness" will be those habits which interfere with the child's life in important ways, either by offending others or by handicapping the child in some other manner. You need not consider a minor habit, with no special consequences for the child with anyone but you, as a symptom of a more basic or serious condition which, unattended to, will at some future time lead to important trouble. It may also simply disappear without attention.

But for "nervousness" that does get the child into trouble by disturbing others or otherwise handicapping her (or him) so that the child is miserable because of it, or deeply disturbed in general, particularly when it includes several symptoms, you can try out any one of many approaches to a solution. You can, for example, look to the child's general physical habits and observe whether eating, sleeping, infection, or illness might be involved, consulting with a physician when you cannot decide. You can try to assess and correct home, school, and play conditions to try to determine whether there is some special source of trouble such as a bullying playmate, a nagging teacher, late home noise that interferes with sleep, or school assignments that cannot be understood.

Generally, however, what is called "nervousness" cannot be pinpointed well or handled on a specific, direct basis. It would seem to be the end-product of a lack of effective structure in the home and/or too many alternatives which the child cannot evaluate, choose among, and pursue systematically and successfully. We believe this because of the "cure" we have often applied successfully to problems of so-called nervousness. What we usually advise and help parents to implement is a better-structured system of control and training in the home so that the child knows what is expected of her, the goals are reasonable for her age and capacities, and she is held to them by a system of rewards. She is treated reasonably, fairly, firmly, consistently, attentively. Almost always, "nervousness" seems to respond to such a firming-up of the child's life, with due attention to reducing choices and distractions, since over-stimulation is another way of viewing the unstructured life of the child that produces the tenseness and uncertainty called "nervousness."

CHAPTER XV

Some Commonly Raised Questions, and Answers, Ages 13-17

THIRTEEN OR SOMEWHAT younger marks the onset of adolescence for girls, while thirteen or somewhat older is the age for most boys. The upper end of the age group discussed here, seventeen, is set at just short of high school graduation, at which point children often leave home, get married, go to college, or take jobs, which usually marks the end of direct and strong parental influence.

The age for relative independence seems, however, to be both lowering and rising in different groups, as an increasing number of children leave home or at least leave the home influence, at fourteen, fifteen, and sixteen; while those who do stay home tend to do so longer as an increasing number go to college and live at home while doing so. If the youth does try to leave home or be present only to sleep, parents who want to insist on determining his way of life can call upon legal officers to bring him home; but if parents want to stop short of so drastic a step, they can usually continue to influence their children away from home by such means as visiting them and controlling funds through making them contingent upon certain living habits.

In any case, parents usually are able to control much less of the behavior of children in this age group than they want to, particularly at the older end. They must use their waning power with care. They have to adapt to the almost independent status of the child, using whatever bonds of affection, money, or other attachment they still possess, to try to influence the child only on the most vital matters. They must get used to the idea that the youth can and should now be almost free of parental ties and able to function independently if he is to make his way effectively as an adult, which he will be expected to do shortly.

1. **Should I make him cut his hair and dress decently?** Several loaded concepts are obvious in the very wording of the question whether you "should make your son cut his hair and dress decently," as so many parents put the problem. "Should" you may really mean "can" you, since you may be practically incapable of getting him to cut his hair without making the break complete between you or using physical force. Then how his hair should be cut, if it is, can be haggled about interminably with no good resolution in sight except for an exact dictum such as schools and military organizations occasionally issue, which can be very detailed and still not cover all the loopholes youngsters can find. And "decent" dress can only mean what the parent likes. It defies any other definition, since clothing styles are tending often to follow what the young people adopt, rather than vice versa.

What the parent seems to be stuck with here is an issue of the degree of independence or conformity that is to be accepted, rather than a precise style that can be exactly defined—if, that is, the parent insists upon a rigid standard for "decency" in dress, instead of the minimum that he can comfortably achieve with his son or daughter. Actually, many parents have become more comfortable with current fads in hair and dress as more adults adopt the youthful styles in both. Long hair and sideburns, beards, beads and pendants, open shirts, military jackets, and pants (on women) have come to be widely worn by university faculty members, advertising people, athletes, and other respectable professionals (not to mention the many parents who have taken to "pot" after being introduced to it by their children).

This question must be referred back, we believe, to the larger question of priorities and where you want to invest your limited time, energy, and influence with your children. Shall this become the overriding issue between you—at the expense, to some extent, of standards for schoolwork, use of money, social activities, honesty, or other goals of your training efforts? If so, you will probably be able to succeed in most cases in getting hair cut (somewhat) and dress modified (to some extent). After all, you have some rewards to utilize for selected purposes, such as use of the car, allowance, and opportunities to work for money, vacations, material possessions. But, with this older age group, you must use such influence sparingly lest your child throw up his arms in despair, disgust, or rage, and simply give up on any reasonable relationship with you or taking any rewards from you.

If the issue for you is in the form of "What will the neighbors (or employers, teachers, relatives, colleagues, or friends) say?" or "What will they think of *me* for letting my child go around like this?" then you are one of millions of parents feeling the same way, and you can share your problems and suffering with your fellow men. The real penalties your child may suffer from his appearance will fall on him more than on you, and he can learn for himself what to do about them. You can wheedle a little and perhaps gain some concessions by offering him new clothes of his own choosing, or by paying for a little hair-cutting, but we are not inclined here to suggest all-out efforts to solve minor or secondary problems and take a chance of masking more important issues for the child's future satisfactions—and yours from him.

2. What time should I make her come home at night? A reasonable hour to come home, and a suitable way to return, can be generally set for your daughter on the basis of her health and safety, as well as her achievement at school. The purpose here should be to keep the hour practical according to these three criteria, rather than setting some theoretical hour of what "seems" to be right from the way your parents raised you or some other such irrelevant consideration.

The safety factor, particularly for your girl, should be based upon realistic possibilities of attack on the route she must take coming home, and whether protective company or safe transportation is available. It might pertain to daylight hours, also, but usually is related to darkness. The health consideration involves how much sleep your child needs to stay well and reasonably rested. The effect on achievement of being home at night is more difficult to separate from other factors involved in accomplishment, but some effort should be made to assess whether the child is home enough to do schoolwork and gets enough sleep to be reasonably alert at school. These same criteria could be used to some extent in assessing the effects of marijuana and other drugs, time spent at play or with friends, and anything else that might interfere with what should be the major concerns of parents in the care and rearing of their children.

No special hour for coming home need be set if not required by any of these standards. It seems inconceivable that one or more of them would *not* be affected if the child frequently got home at two or three A.M. But the criteria should always be foremost, and the hour to return home be set accordingly. Then the same principles of reward and penalty as discussed throughout the book would be assessed, the rewards in this case consisting of privileges. That is, use of the car would be contingent upon being home by a certain hour, and the offer of its use withdrawn for a week or two if the hour is not observed. School grades would have to be maintained at a reasonable level (and checked on more often than by semesters), or more evenings would have to be reserved for studying.

What is the parent to do if the child continues to violate the rules when they have been carefully drawn? We have never yet exhausted in our clinical practices the possibilities for improving rules and rewards until they work adequately to achieve the goals. By careful planning, patience, and persistence, and firmness about implementation but flexibility about experimentation, the parent can, we believe, bring the problem under control. If he should become desperate, however, he should seek expert help (or change to a different source of help), or call upon the legal or social agencies of the community to assist in implementing reasonable processes.

3. **How can I be sure that she doesn't smoke, drink, or use drugs?** You cannot ever be certain that your daughter (or son) does not smoke, drink, or use drugs, and the reason is crucial to our discussion here. It is because you cannot monitor your daughter's behavior, at this age, all the time. She will be at places and with people at times when you cannot observe or get reports on her, and it is futile to hope for complete information about her either by conversation with her or by your investigations. The best you can do, therefore, is to make your views known as clearly as possible, and to discuss them with her as often as you can, listening to her views in the process and learning from them; to be alert to observing signs of usage whenever you can, and forbidding it in your presence or home (if you are against it), and enforcing the rules effectively; to be consistent in your words and deeds about it (either by yourself not indulging, or by telling her it is

all right for her to do so when she reaches a specified age).

You can and should intervene, of course, when her health is involved or important areas of her life disrupted, as when she cannot study because of a hangover, when she has a chronic hoarseness or sore throat, when she walks around in a daze, unresponsive to things around her, when she is uncontrollably restless or aggressive. At such a point, of course, you must insist upon treatment of some kind, including hospitalization if she she will not accept other forms. Short of this, however, and in the overwhelming number of cases, the results of drug usage are undramatic, often undetectable and, as much as for your generation, perhaps, not seriously damaging. In these latter cases, if you are to make usage a moral or value judgment, you must be consistent about it to give your purpose serious merit in your child's eyes, and then use the same kind of reward and penalty system you would use for any other kind of objective of your training efforts.

We will not repeat the reward and penalty suggestions here, since they are covered elsewhere in this chapter—use of car, opportunities to host friends and have parties, special privileges of other sorts. But one special consideration should be mentioned in connection with drug usage—that of helping the youth to develop alternative sources of pleasure. Many dancers and athletes, for example, do not use drugs because they interfere with their most important activities. Similarly for those who become highly involved in art, writing, skilled mechanical work, driving, or flying. This fact gives us perhaps the key to the control of drug usage in the youth. That is, to make it our primary training goal to help the child in all the various ways discussed to develop the discipline and other skills necessary to gain a sense of fulfillment. This is perhaps the most effective antidote to a sense of futility or the pursuit of a simple and shortsighted hedonism that enhances the susceptibility to drug abuse.

4. **Should I let him drive as soon as he legally can?** Three reasons are commonly given by the parent who does *not* want his child to learn to drive as soon as he reaches the legal age: the parent may be too "nervous" to let his young son (or daughter) drive because of the dangers involved to the child—or to the car; the parent may label the son an incompetent who is not ready yet (when he *will* be ready is seldom predicted); or the parent holds grievances against the son and punishes him by not letting him learn to drive.

Learning to drive *can* be a joyful experience in the relationship of parent to son or daughter (it is, in any case, to the youth, and why should the parent not seek to share it?). It is a wonderful privilege the parent can offer his child, which would naturally develop happily if the parent did not load the situation with troubles from outside sources. The parent's nervousness about the child's driving should never, of course, be allowed to interfere with the child's development toward maturity. This is the parent's problem, for which he should seek help. But there might be help enough for it if he would only steel himself to let the child learn to drive in spite of the parent's worry. It is likely that the parent will get used to this development if he will simply force himself to experience it—the same as he gets used to the child's going to school, going out to parties, or taking an airplane trip. It is likely also that the parent will never, merely by forcing the child to wait for some unspecified time before being allowed to drive, find it easier to face the problem just because some months or years have elapsed.

Labeling the child incompetent to drive is merely to state a problem, not to suggest a solution—unless it is to be sure that the child learns as well as possible so that he does not remain incompetent. For the child to be called "too nervous," "too impulsive," or "too scatterbrained" to drive, and to leave him without hope of driving, would seem to condemn him to lifelong inadequacy in the parent's eyes and perhaps his own in this regard. How much better to seek a solution by trying to train him in stability, concentration, and skill in the area of driving at least! Finally, to punish the child by forbidding him to drive—for past sins, and without a specific termination date—is to make him feel hopeless and unredeemable.

Obviously, then, we are suggesting a forward-looking handling of the driving problem, making it a privilege the child can look forward to and happily begin as soon as he is legally able. After the child learns to drive and can be trusted with the car for errands and personal pleasure, it will be probably the most powerful reward you can offer him for meeting household responsibilities, handling his schoolwork well, and conducting himself reasonably in society. You should never forego such an opportunity to utilize his interests and desires for training him toward maturity.

5. **What if she hates me?** Hate in children is more freely and spontaneously expressed than in adults, and therefore does not connote as much desperation or permanence as it does when it is suppressed, veiled, or indirectly expressed. By adolescence, however, the child is often feeling shame or guilt about it, particularly with regard to parents, and particularly with those many parents who act horrified, crushed, or ashamed when their children express it.

If you could simply listen to expressions of anger as natural outbursts against you for frustrating the child, often having about the same function as swearing does for you when you trip on a rock, you would be able to do your job as a parent objectively without getting involved in the child's emotion, remaining steady with your training objectives and methods.

The assessment of this emotion, with any others the youth expresses (but this one is perhaps the most disturbing to parents), needs to be in terms of how intense and long-lasting it is. The expression of hate, which is usually an outburst from being frustrated in getting what he wants and which passes over in a matter of hours, can be patiently ignored by the parent who feels confident about his own behavior with his child. He has no reason to feel devastated by such expressions, as if they were thunderbolts of judgment upon him from Heaven. They are merely natural, thoughtless, and harmless outbursts of children.

Expressions of hatred which are intense to the point of disrupting the youth's life, or which last for weeks or months, are another matter. They suggest a serious problem in the relationship between parent and youth. If they are rewarding to the youth because, when he talks this way, the parent becomes miserable and abjectly tries to give his child whatever he wants, they are serving the youth's purposes well, and he is unwittingly being trained by the parent to use them as a method for getting what he wants. Obviously such expressions should not be rewarded. Beyond that, the parent should talk with child and others to try to determine whether he is giving the child good cause for such feelings and, if so, how to function better as a parent. Assuming, however, that you are a well-intentioned parent and not in that small minority who may hate and reject their children and engender the same spirit in return from their children, we believe that continued expressions of this sort in the child probably stem from ineffectual methods of training on your part. That is, unclear and unspecified goals for the child, inconsistency in your training procedures, uncertain rewards and penalties, conflicts between parents in the process—all need to be reviewed in the light of the principles and procedures discussed elsewhere in this book, so that the child can gain a stronger sense of purpose and efficacy about your role and his own.

6. **What can I do about foul language?** "Foul" language is a constantly shifting thing. "God" was used as a nasty expletive generations ago, and in the more recent past so was "damn," but most parents would gladly exchange either or both for others which have become popular today. Since words harm no one and your child is not likely to use the same language when applying for a job or reciting at school as he does with his classmates, you can more safely ignore this pecadillo than others we are discussing in this chapter. Since age should confer no special privileges here, if you are going to criticize and try to shape his speech, you must be sure of your own, and set him the example you want him to learn. If he continues, in your presence, to use language he knows you disapprove of—and your first step is, of course, to make your attitudes clear—you can assume that he is either deliberately flaunting his freedom of speech, speaking as spontaneously with you as with his friends, or intentionally taunting you.

Your problem here is mainly to decide how high a priority to give to trying to change his behavior in this regard, as compared with the many other ways you might want to train him in. You cannot work on all of his behavior at once, so you must decide what is most important. If you decide that this area is of high importance, you should try to shape it in all the ways we have already described, involving any of the rewards and penalties at your disposal.

More simply, however, and reflecting our own preference, we would suggest that you try to handle the situation only through your direct conversations with him, by refusing to discuss his requests unless he tries to conform at least minimally to your wishes in the use of language and other common courtesies. This is your most effective and immediate tool for shaping his behavior without getting involved in moralistic judgments, academic arguments, or general condemnations of his friends and manners. You would merely be requiring him to recognize and learn to conform to some sort of model for speech you approve of, whenever he wants something from you. It is likely that this will affect his behavior in other settings also, however.

7. **How can I get him to do things with us as a family?** It is not so much a question of how to get him to do things—anything—with you as a family, as how to get him to do things *you* want him to do with you all. Obviously if you pick activities that he wants very very much to do, and he can do them *only* with you as a family, he is quite likely to participate in such family activities. He is likely to go skiing with the family in Michigan or Colorado if that is the only way he can get support for a ski trip away from home. He is also likely to go with you to Europe, to stay at a lake cabin, to drive the car, if doing so as a family is the only way open to him to do these things—and if the family is not totally malfunctioning or objectionable to him. If, however, you ask him, as a matter of duty, to go with the family to church, to attend a party of relatives or your adult friends, to shop for groceries, or to ski nearby—and he prefers, naturally, the company of his friends in these or other activities—then you must have outside rewards to promise him for doing things with the family that he wants to do.

He may, with age, decide to do a few things with the family for sentimental or duty reasons, such as church-going or attending a gathering of relatives, but for you to exhort him to stay with the family because he *should* enjoy it is usually to make a futile appeal. It is more realistic to indicate that it is your pleasure rather than his that is involved. While this is a legitimate appeal, its effectiveness will depend upon your good relationship with him, which should, in turn, be rewarding to him. You get into a battle when you say he *should*, and imply that he should *want* to, when clearly he has no interest and probably should not, finding younger siblings often a "drag," parents and their generation often a bore, and having much more pleasure in being with his friends. You would be more rational to put your appeal on the basis of occasionally pleasing you, or promising some privilege he does want in exchange for the discharge of a kind of parent-imposed requirement.

8. **How can I be sure she won't get into trouble with the boys she dates?** You can never be sure that your daughter will not get into trouble with a boy she dates. You cannot monitor the activities of an adolescent girl sufficiently to keep her safe from sexual relations or the introduction to drugs, which are likely to be the parent's main concern for a daughter. And there is very little use in trying to interrogate your daughter constantly about where she has been and with whom. She will tell you the truth only if her relationship with you is good, not because you are always nagging her. The hour of three to four P.M. in the boy's parents' empty house is as convenient for intercourse as midnight to one A.M. in his car, and much less likely to be questioned by you. It is futile, in other words, to try to extend your direct control to the adolescent's life as you would to the younger child's.

This is not to say that you should not express your interest and concern and make your own values and goals specific and clear. You need for this purpose to have some principles concerning sex and drug usage that you feel confident about, to discuss with your child. You will hope that your daughter (or son) will come to accept and practice—eventually—some values and goals such as you profess, and this probably will happen—eventually. Meanwhile, however, she will experiment and modify her opinions on the basis of her experiences, and you can only try to make these experiences as safe for her as possible—physically, legally, and psychologically.

We have already discussed in this chapter the problem of drug usage, and will confine ourselves here to the problem of sexual relations in adolescence. In degrees of traumatic consequences of sexual play in adolescence, one must start with pregnancy, and the basic precaution the parent should exercise is to be sure that her daughter is informed specifically about the necessity and methods of birth control. You really have no other rational choice in this matter. Whether the information will be encouraging intercourse, or whether your daughter will reject it or find it offensive cannot be given overriding consideration. Ignorance is simply not a very good alternative to choose, in order to keep your daughter out of trouble; yet that is what you would be chancing if you were not to educate your daughter about sex and birth control.

It is extremely important also that you keep communications about sex as free and full as possible so that your daughter will have maximum opportunity to discuss her developing relationships with you. You can thus have the chance to influence her behavior. You will have, however, few rewards to offer that will be at all commensurate with the pleasures inherent in sexual relationships. You will, therefore, have to depend here, more than in other areas of behavior, upon the relationship between you, the influence of your principles upon your child's behavior, and perhaps (if your daughter gives you the opportunity) the chance to affect her choice of male companions and her opportunities to find pleasure and interest in other activities. The best antidote to precocious concentration on sexual activities is strong competing interests.

9. What can I do about his friends whom I don't like? Into and after adolescence it is almost impossible for the parent to control the son's (or daughter's) choice of friends. Whatever influence he has been able to exercise and whatever direction he has been able to set have usually occurred at earlier ages. Now the child is largely on his own, in environments that the parent can seldom observe—in fact, may be largely unaware of. You may not like what you do see of your son's friends, but you should be as sure as you can that your opinion is based upon your firsthand knowledge of these friends rather than some casual observation of their hair or dress or some casual conversation you may have overheard. It therefore would be desirable for you to try to talk with your son's friends. If you have any respect for your son, you should at least be curious about what he sees in his friends. Chances are you will often end up with more favorable opinions than your first perhaps unfavorable impressions.

You can also try to influence his exposure to those who are potential friends, although you will have a much harder time of it now than at earlier ages. You can, for example, invite youths from out of town, or even from abroad, whom you may meet in contacts you can develop with youth activities, over the holidays and other special occasions when your son will be present. You can invite him to have as house guests or on family trips, or offer to pay for entertainment tickets for, those friends or acquaintances of his who you think would make the most desirable companions for him. Often, however, your judgments will be much more superficial and misinformed than his.

Mostly, you will have to accept his choice of friends and work from there to affect, as you can, his attitudes, behavior, and values with them. It is important also that you maintain as effective communication with your son as you can with regard to his companions, so that he will not be afraid of or angered by your critical opinions to the point that he ceases to discuss his friends with you. When communication ceases, so does the best possibility of your exercising influence in this area.

10. **How can I get her to eat decently?** To train her in good eating habits at this age, after all the earlier years when she was exposed to far more powerful influence from you, is extremely difficult and must, practically, be limited to basic and minimal considerations of health and courtesy. That is, she has a great deal of freedom about what, indeed whether, she eats at school at lunch time, or at a friend's house at dinnertime, or on trips away from home, or when she comes home after the family mealtime because of legitimate activities away from home, and this makes it generally futile for the parent to try to control or train eating habits.

The only behavior the parent can continue to try to shape involves the basics of health and courtesy that he can directly observe. That is, if the daughter gets obviously too thin or fat for her health, the parent should exercise control—but control based less than when the child is younger on the exact eating habits at the table (although it may come to that if health is endangered), and more upon the observable outcome. That is, if your daughter can, on her own, gain sufficient control to eat more or less, as the situation demands, that can be the end of the matter. If, however, she does not show results over several months, it is time to tighten up on the mealtime pattern. You should structure the situation by insisting, for example, that she be home for all possible meals and eat with you, where she can be observed. You can offer her a new wardrobe if she loses or gains weight, as the need may be, or a trip or some other prized reward when she reaches a desired goal. Also smaller rewards for shorter term objectives should be established, which might involve checking weight weekly or more often.

The other matter, courtesy at the table, should be observed and handled like other habits discussed in this chapter. You will, of course, be insisting on certain manners only for your own satisfaction, since you will have little chance to observe and influence her behavior in most eating situations outside the home. You can do this by using the methods discussed in previous sections of this chapter.

11. **Should I let him have his own car when it is legal?** There are financial, use, and distraction problems to be considered in deciding whether to let your son own a car. The first question to be asked is what the car is wanted for. For various financial and other practical reasons, there would seem to be no reason to permit a car, which can distract an adolescent from his schoolwork and toward earning money to keep it up, unless there is some overriding positive gain from having it. Good reasons for the youth to have a car might, of course, exist. It might be necessary for transportation to a special school or for participation in some especially desirable outside activity which the parent wants to support; it might permit him to work—which should have some special merit beyond simply providing for the support of the car; it might permit him to provide special services to the family such as transporting others to school, lessons, or work when these others cannot drive themselves.

None of these reasons requires that your son own the car, however. That would have no special merit in these situations, and it would include the disadvantages of requiring more costly insurance than if you owned the car and reducing your control over its use. Owning his own car would have to distract him from his schoolwork also, although that could be controlled by insisting that he take care of his main tasks before being allowed use of the car—or even allowed to retain it. Car ownership might have merit if it encouraged him to work and save his money— provided this could be done without harm to his school- work; or if he had special mechanical interests and aptitudes which were focused on and developed by ownership of a car.

12. What if she insists on leaving home when she is fifteen? To have a daughter announce that she is leaving home, whether specifying whom she is going to live with or not saying, is only slightly less traumatic to Mother than having her declare that she is going off to share a room with her boyfriend.

At what age and under what conditions should you try to adapt to the idea of your daughter's leaving home to live her own life? Hardly any parent could or should accept such a break with home in twelve-, thirteen-, or fourteen-year-olds. By fifteen or sixteen, the line is more blurred, but by seventeen or eighteen probably most parents would accept the departure, perhaps reluctantly, probably only with strongly stated reservations and conditions. And how could you do otherwise when many youth will be finishing their highest schooling, getting married, or leaving home for college or jobs at eighteen?

Ages fifteen and sixteen represent perhaps the period of most severe conflict and uncertainty today. When viewed as a matter of only slight prematurity at most, the question can be considered most rationally. Such perspective should mean that, at least under some specifiable conditions which are favorable, the year or two involved before most parents would accept the break, could be skipped. Besides, there are great differences in youth of this age in physical and psychological maturity, so that your daughter might easily be able to function as well at fifteen as the average seventeen- or eighteen-year-old, if she is exceptional. In the intellectual area, this would require an I.Q. of around 115, 120, or above.

If you have developed and maintained an effective system of communication up to this age, and a system of rewards as previously discussed, you can use your influence, judiciously, to keep your child under reasonable controls. But you may also have to adapt. Above all it is important to keep channels of communication open between you so that you can continue to exercise *some* influence at least. You should never allow yourself to be pinned into a corner where you disown your child or try to cut yourself off entirely if she does such and such. Chances are you won't be able to do this even if you try to, and will regret and have to modify whatever ultimatums you deliver that reject her entirely.

When all else fails by way of communication and reward system for what your goals would ordinarily be, you will be confronted with the desirability of conserving any slight control and influence you retain by evaluating as fully as you can just what living conditions your daughter is proposing and trying to affect them to any extent you can, even if you must compromise considerably. You should be willing and prepared to put at least as much into the negotiations as management and labor do with each other for much less intense emotional and personal reasons. You would try to make the roommates and living conditions as favorable from your standpoint as you can—by such means as offers of financial help, furnishings, nearby location, whatever is available to you to offer and have her consider. Above all, you should maintain communication. Even if you do not approve of the departure, and strongly disapprove of the companions and quarters, you can retain some modicum of influence simply by maintaining as close contact as remains feasible.

INDEX